PLAYGROUNDS
OF OUR MINDS

PLAYGROUNDS OF OUR MINDS

John Barell
Montclair State College

Teachers College, Columbia University
New York and London 1980

Copyright © 1980 by Teachers College, Columbia University.
All rights reserved. Published by Teachers College Press, 1234
Amsterdam Avenue, New York, NY 10027.

Library of Congress Cataloging in Publication Data

Barell, John.
  Playgrounds of our minds.

  Bibliography: p.
  Includes index.
    1. Creative thinking (Education) 2.   Fantasy.
  3. Play. 4.   Education, Secondary—United States—
  Curricula. I.   Title.
  LB1062.B37   370.15'2   79-27084
  ISBN 0-8077-2580-3

Designed by Romeo Enriquez
1 2 3 4 5 6 7 8   87 86 85 84 83 82 81 80
Manufactured in the U.S.A.

*For all persons who
Help us build the
Playgrounds of our lives,
Especially Nancy Ann.*

CONTENTS

FOREWORD

THE IMPORTANCE OF PLAY in human existence has been noted by perceptive thinkers over and over again, both in the contexts of human development and of the quality of existence.

Our present culture or modern consciousness, as Peter Burger puts it, is one which does not emphasize play. We are a serious or serial culture, where work and technical rationality are prized above their cultural competitors or alternatives. The Protestant work ethic, or its Marxian alternative, work philosophy, seem securely imbedded in the "modern consciousness."

Thus, the very qualities of play—the active aesthetic and moral meanings of the immediate endeavor, the signs of transcendence in play, the lack of concern for means-end relationships, and immersion in the present—are denied their role in human life by seriality and seriousness of our present cultural thrust.

That this culture enters into the human living of schools is eloquently and adequately detailed in our educational studies. Separation of work and play is well established early in kindergarten, and soon work is seen as the more important of the two activities, as the kind of activity fostered and prized by the school.

John Barell's book may be seen as a partial antidote to this poisonous concept of preemptive work in our schools.

At last, we have a work which removes play from frivolity or "child's activity" and puts it directly into human and curricular meanings. As Barell shows, "play" or "playfulness" are integral and needed aspects of school activity.

It is, in fact, the potentially playful and creative aspects of schooling that are most often ignored or deliberately repressed through routine school practice.

We should be indebted to Dr. Barell for writing such a lucid and well developed approach to play in schooling and for the clarity of his specific illustrations and examples. We have long needed and awaited the re-emergence of play in the curriculum in its integrated functionality. Dr. Barell's contribution will open this door for us.

JAMES B. MACDONALD
Distinguished Professor of Education
University of North Carolina

ACKNOWLEDGEMENTS

A BOOK IS LIKE a ship sailing into unknown waters, and there are many whose interest and concern helped launch this one. Gary Griffin, teacher and colleague, initially suggested I undertake the task. Several teachers read the text and offered very thoughtful suggestions: Ruth Penner, Harriet Rosenstein, Sarah McGinty, George Magdich, Harry Ahearn, John Golebiewski, Steve Meili, Joe Moore, Cliff Knapp, Evan Maletsky, and especially Don Maiocco. Without the cooperation of the principal and teachers of David's and Laura's school, I would never have become acquainted with the six persons whose imaginativeness made this book such an adventure: Tim, Gordon, Bob, Betsy, Lisa, and Marie. My editor, Mary L. Allison, provided me with much assistance, and her delight in the playfulness of young people has been most encouraging. And Ivan Homola whose sensitivity to self-fulfillment and the spirit of play helped set the keel for this vessel.

J.B.

INTRODUCTION

ONE OF MY FAVORITE playgrounds is located in New York City's Central Park. It was designed by Richard Dattner and is composed of hills, slides, tunnels, rope climbs, rubber tire swings, and tree huts, all surrounded by shifting sands that ebb and flow about children and their toys like a small sea. I often sit and watch the kids laughing and frolicking over the hills, climbing and swinging on knotted ropes, sliding down metal slides, running across the vast expanses of sand and up a nearby tree to perch and peer from the wooden scaffolding encircling its trunk at a height of about ten feet. From high above the rippling sands I hear kids proclaim themselves Captain Fantastic or Superwoman and whiz off to conquer imaginary worlds of their own creation, worlds separated from those of their adult companions by a low cement wall. When they have rescued the innocent from certain death, or have grown tired, or have been beckoned home for the tenth time, the children crawl through a tunnel in the wall and re-enter the adult world and its reality.

When these children grow up and go to secondary school, they will still play; their playgrounds are more likely to be the inner spaces of their minds where in their daydreams they imagine untested possibilities and pretend to be doctors, generals, sports heroes, or sensitive, conquering lovers.

For children and adolescents play is a freely chosen activity where they control the roles and events of playing superhero or "What I'll do when I grow up" in ways not always possible in the real world. In addition to freedom and control, play is characterized by imaginative transformation of reality in accordance with our wishes and dreams for as long as we please. Children as well as teenagers and adults play by imitating other people, cracking jokes, building hideouts, and pretending to be space travelers zooming through the cosmos at the speed of light. The difference is that as we grow older the rope and sand playgrounds are slowly transformed into playgrounds of our minds, those boundless stages upon which we entice, thrust, and parade a host of characters who endlessly act out novel solutions to original problems.

The premise of this book is that play is a natural activity for all human beings and that it enhances our physical, social, emotional, and intellectual growth and development from one stage of life to another. In play we learn about ourselves and our world, while occasionally engaging in emotionally stressing situations. Through our play we perpetually generate novelty; play, observed Sutton-Smith (1975) "potentiates novelty" and increases our adaptability to a world of constant change. Play is not the same thing as creativity; the former is often ephemeral, episodic, and nondirective, whereas the latter demands a rigor and sense of direction to produce a final product, be it a painting, a formula, or a story.

The link between play and what occurs in schools is its foundation in the imagination. Imagination is the ability to transcend the immediate reality of sitting here at my typewriter and to "see" myself teaching tonight, to feel certain emotions related to that image, and to toy with the possibilities of how to teach what. In schools teachers and students think, act, and feel their way into various subjects that are founded upon man's ability to imagine what is not present. Numbers, letters, words, pictures, stories of people real and imagined, scientific formulae—all have had their origin in the playgrounds of the minds of Euclid, Einstein, Hemingway, or Leonardo. Playing on such playgrounds is, I think, a prerequisite to all productive thought in any area of human inquiry or endeavor.

Another link between play and schools is the similarity between what occurs on the Dattner playground and in classrooms—a continual creation and reaction to novelty. No two play episodes and no two teaching-learning events are the same; in both playgrounds and classrooms people act with interest, freedom, and control when confronting an original situation. One unfortunate difference is that in teaching too often teachers' responses become encrusted and embedded in routine because they gradually close themselves off to the novelty of the situations, to the serendipities inherent in how each student thinks and feels. Perhaps conceiving of ourselves as players on a playground will help teachers maintain some of their openness to the mystery and beauty of the human mind and its imaginative powers.

To exemplify the playfulness of boys and girls and to help teachers understand its nature I have formed an artistic composite of three different boys in the character of David and three different girls in the person of Laura. These are students I have lived with in classrooms, observed in sports, clubs, and social activities after school, and with whom I have taken several expeditions to winter camping sites and rural communes. Because these portraits are composites of several different individuals, they may seem unrealistic, and it might appear that I have forgotten the more passive, nonverbal child who sits next to David or Laura or who is pestered by them occasionally. As a friend commented after reading about David and Laura, "Sometimes I feel they play and take away from the others." This will be true at times. However, my point in focusing upon them is that they exemplify in a heightened sense the imaginative potential of most adolescents. Consequently, I have searched for the best examples as illustrations.

Why might play and playfulness be significant? What evidence is there that play and playfulness are significant human activities? My answers derive from my knowledge of childhood and adolescent development, recent studies of successful adult living, the lives of productive thinkers, and from how high school students play in and out of class all the time.

We know that children's imaginative play is affected by the time, toys, space, and importance of this activity within a culture. Children who are taught to play by adults show improvement in their abilities to think innovatively; they are verbally more flexible and fluent and are more empathic in their relations with friends. Not all children play the same game with the same amount of imaginative investment in the roles they create and the problems they solve, but within the right environment children's play can be enhanced and made more imaginative.

The developmental theories of Jean Piaget and Erik Erikson provide ways of understanding the social-emotional and intellectual play described in this volume. Erikson (1974) sees adolescence as a stage of growth characterized by social role play, "the genetic successor of childhood play." Through experimentation and risk taking they play out in reality and fantasy some of the roles imagined and enacted in the Central Park playground. Indeed, returning to this playground recently I found myself sporting about the ladders and tree climbs reliving some of my adolescent fantasies of what I might become in adulthood. Most of us can do this, because by adolescence we begin to think more abstractly and can imagine ourselves as composites of real and imaginary persons; we can project ourselves into the future and see ourselves as captains of interstellar space craft; we can accept impossible hypotheses ("What if the earth began to rotate in the opposite direction?") and consider the possible consequences. Piaget called this ability "formal operations," a quality of thinking different from the more concrete mental operations of children in elementary schools (Inhelder, 1958).

Having spent the past two years observing students in classrooms, I have noticed the many and varied ways they play just to avoid boredom or doing what the teacher has asked them to do: daydreaming, doodling, toying with glass cases and venetian blind cords, game playing such as "get the teacher off the topic," story telling, and writing messages to friends on paper and on desks. These are all considered "off-task" by teachers, but fun, important, and meaningful by the students. Ignoring these activities, which to me are imaginative in nature because they solve a problem for a student in a novel way, overlooks a useful and developable skill and interest.

Recent longitudinal studies of male development (Levinson, 1978) have attempted to isolate the transitional phases as well as to indicate some of the successful coping mechanisms used to establish healthy relations with others, have a good self-understanding, and work with happiness. One observer (Vaillant, 1977) has identified these "mature defense mechanisms" requisite to successful adaptation: suppression, humor, altruism, anticipation and sublimation. It seems to me that, at a minimum, humor, altruism, and anticipation require imaginative activity. Altruism, especially, suggests the empathic skills and attitudes Martin Buber (1965) called the ability to "imagine the real" situation of another person, and this is developed through the ability to play in a variety of roles throughout life.

And, finally, we know something about the importance of imaginative skills within a playful context from two other sources: the thought processes of productive thinkers and some research on developing these very skills. In discussing how he thought about a problem, Einstein said, "The physical entities which seem to serve as elements in thought are certain signs and more or less clear images which can be 'voluntarily' reproduced and combined. . . . This combinatory play seems to be the essential feature in productive thought—before there is any connection with logical construction in words or other kinds of signs which can be communicated to others" (Koestler, 1964, p. 171). Playing with ideas was essential before Einstein began to think logically and more rigorously. His *gedanken,* or thought experiments, are good examples of this toying with ideas.

Combinatory play with ideas might also be called daydreaming and fantasizing. Recent research by Singer (1976) indicates that there is a demonstrable correlation between the strength of adolescents' inner resources and some of their acting out behaviors, which might be antisocial.

These, then, are some reasons why I think it is desirable to focus upon adolescent imaginative behavior as exemplified in their play, a voluntary open-ended activity pursued for its own sake, and in their playfulness, an approach to life that arises out of play experiences.

Playgrounds is not a book of "how-to" recipes. Readers are expected to act imaginatively upon the content suggested and not attempt to transfer activities word for word into their classrooms. Explore, test, reconstruct, and pretend in the smithy of your own imagination. The ideas presented in each chapter, hopefully, are fruitful enough to stimulate the imaginations of teachers in every discipline, and you are urged to read beyond the subjects you personally teach to explore other mysteries.

Furthermore, the activities proposed in *Playgrounds* reflect a way of looking at the classroom, at adolescents whose imaginations are too often overlooked, and at a curriculum that provides inadequate openings for personal expressiveness. David made a charming and somewhat derisive comment about the curriculum he lived through in a story he wrote for the fun of it entitled "The Mystical Volcano of Heineken," a tale describing the world of high school students known as The Land of Whoopie. Inhabitants of Whoopie were given to having continuous parties to which Dischord, the God of the Five Paragraph Expository Essay, was not invited. Incensed perhaps by the lack of structure, the absence of logical thinking neatly divided into five segments complete with topic statements supported efficiently by examples, facts, or statistics, Dischord

> . . . was mad. "I shall gather together all of my Freshmen, and I shall destroy their entire planet!" he cackled insanely. One bad wazoo that guy. In less than a millenium (gods live for a long, long time, and *never* go to bed early) Dischord and his bloodthirsty Freshmen, who were crazed by tales of high school life, attacked the peaceful planet of Whoopie en masse. . . . Singing and swigging, every native of Whoopie found a Freshman, and plied him with berry juice until his beady little eyes glazed over. Then they stole the Freshman's schedules (no freshman can exist for more than a few hours without a schedule telling him what period it is), and threw them all into the Volcano of Heineken where they were reduced to cinders. . . . Dischord, God of the Five Paragraph Expository Essay, was beaten and he barely escaped with his life and his red marking pencil (Ritter, 1978).

Playgrounds does not laud the defeat of the God of the Five Paragraph Suppository Essay, as one of David's friends called it, nor does it wish to institutionalize or ritualize that which already exists, that is, student drinking habits. It does intend, however, to say that inhabitants of Whoopie are too often forced to constrain and inhibit their fun-loving and playful imaginations. The irony of the name Dischord results from the fact that the five paragraph expository essay symbolizes, for me, the convergent-upon-an-accepted-answer kinds of analytic thinking and didactic teaching that are really quite different from the disharmonies of an active imagination. But both are portions of an integral whole: the logical, cause and effect, sequential thinking of the scientist needs to be balanced by the idiosyncratic pretending, dreaming, free associating, and novelty production of the artist. Productive thinking incorporates both art and science, imagination and logical thought, Whoopie and the five paragraph expository essay.

The Land of Whoopie represents and is a product of the human imagination that created the subjects studied in schools and that can act upon content—the knowledge, skills, and attitudes—thus creating more personal meaningfulness. Such meaningfulness results from playing upon the fields of Whoopie and thinking about such questions as, "What if all atoms were inhabited by intelligent beings?" When David responded, "The word 'it' would have a different meaning," he found new perspectives on the words he uses; when Laura answered, "Maybe we on earth are just an atom in the body of some giant," she was developing a new hypothesis from the original imaginative question.

Finding new ways of looking at the world, new meanings, and developing our abstract thinking capabilities are two of the rewards of playing with ideas. We know that not all adolescents and adults are equally adept at what Piaget calls formal, abstract thinking (Mosher, 1979); we also know that growth in the ability to see possibilities, generate hypotheses, and deduce consequences is possible. *Playgrounds* provides some imaginative frameworks for developing these productive thinking skills. In pondering the possibility of life in the atom, David and Laura were again building sand castles and solving the problems of charging cowboys and escaping Indians, just as they were projecting themselves into their own unknown futures with their nearly unlimited choices for career, love relationships, and geographical space.

In the end, nothing suggested here denigrates what is termed the basics—composing, computing, and comprehending. Rather it enhances students' growth and development as thinking and feeling individuals who are defining themselves and determining their futures. If educators focus as much upon development as upon achievement, it seems to me that David would be less likely to say, as he did to me once, "It's a shame that school has interrupted my education."

Narrowing this gap between schooling and education may be one result of David's and Laura's being encouraged to act more imaginatively upon the content that is thrust upon them.

PLAYGROUNDS
OF OUR MINDS

1

DAVID AND LAURA IN THE LAND OF WHOOPIE

DAVID DANCED INTO chemistry a minute late as usual as if onto a stage where he was the only player, looked about for the teacher, Mr. Stump, and noticing his absence snuck up on Laura, his very attractive lab mate who was standing near her oxidation experiment apparatus. With one foot slowly placed in front of the other, arms outstretched like a high wire expert, David suddenly clamped his chin on her shoulder.

"God!" she shrieked, just barely managing to prevent her pipette from slipping out of her wet hands and onto the floor.

"No, just me," smiled David bending around and looking up at Laura's chagrined face.

"Jeez, David, you almost made me drop this thing! And I'd have to pay for it!" She looked a little angry as she hid the pipette and started on her math calculations. "Why're you goofin' *all* the time anyway?"

"Goofin's more fun. Where'd you get the new calculator?" he asked taking a piece of paper from her notebook.

"My birthday. . .yesterday—"

"Ooooohhhh!" he sang in a high pitched voice. He then stepped back, bowed slightly at the waist, and with a wave of his hand and

1

a broad smile revealing his never-had-a-cavity white teeth led three onlooking students in a rapid chorus of "Happy Birthday to You."

Laura beamed and added a slow soft shoe routine she had learned for such spontaneous occasions. "Thank you, thank you, one and all," she said to some applause. "But David, I can't figure out the scale on this thing."

"Oh, well, let me see." He took the calculator and reared his head back in jest at the instrument staring coldly at him. "What scales *you?*" he asked in the *basso profundo* professorial tones he often used to mock the scientific method.

"The *scale,* David!"

"Oh, yeah." David cleared his throat with annoying stridency. "Mary, had a little Lamb, little Lamb, little Lamb," crooned David to his imaginary audience. "No, wait a minute—it's a C Minor scale, if I remember correctly." Now scratching his head to generate a third alternative, "Perhaps you've got a biorhythm scale here Laura, my dear."

Espying Mr. Stump entering the classroom with casual self-assuredness, Laura and David took their seats next to each other.

"Does anybody have.any questions about yesterday's lesson?" No one raised a hand so Laura, after a pregnant pause of sufficient duration, grinned and popped a question. She had begun to play her game of "have you ever imagined. . . ?"

"Mr. Stump, sir, what do you suppose would happen if our world were really just one of the billions of atoms in the universe of some giant? Ya know, what if we are really an atom in the body of some fantastically large creature?"

"Yeah," retorted David, "and all the rain outside is just the sweat from under his hairy arms?"

"No, no, you guys," laughed Margie, "What if every atom in *our* bodies was a miniature universe or Milky Way?" By now the class was beginning to think this was fun.

"And all our viruses are really comets racing between several universes," chortled Roger waving his hand through airy space.

"O.K., O.K., boys and girls, enough fun and games for now. Maybe we really are just part of some giant's body," he said with a slight grin. "If so, I do hope we in this class are located somewhere near the brain, though at times I *do* have my doubts about some of you." He looked over the tops of his horn rimmed glasses in David and Laura's direction. Turning around he proceeded behind his large demonstration desk raised almost a foot off the floor. "Let's try to be serious about the problems of atomic weight shall we? Those giants with sweaty armpits exist only in your imaginations." And the class waddled onto the periodic table.

It may be true that such giants and micro-universes exist within the imaginations of very playful people like David and Laura. Whether or not to entertain the possibilities Laura posed was a values question her teacher decided to place a low priority upon for more pressing matters—the need to cover specific factual information in a short period of time, a pressure situation all teachers face. The unfortunate aspect of Mr. Stump's rejection was that Laura and David and their friends were toying with possibilities on a grandiose, if seemingly illogical, scale, and this toying was what Einstein called "combinatory play with ideas," a necessary prerequisite to the more logical, cause and effect thinking often identified with science. However, both play and rigor are necessary for productive thought. Playing with ideas is at the very heart of the creative process; it reflects the basic relationship between science and imagination, and, more importantly, between the imagination and all human ways of knowing and doing.

The basic thesis of this book is that science, like all other disciplines, is founded upon the imagination, and imaginative thinking is an undervalued skill in the lives of most adolescents and educators. It is perhaps an undervalued approach to life on the part of many human beings. The playful people I have studied in their schools, playgrounds, and homes exemplify some of the imaginative activities that, I believe, are fundamental to learning, thinking, and doing in all the traditional subject areas. The mind of man is the quintessential playground within which we play an infinite variety of roles, enact myriad possible courses of action, resolve scores of problems, toy with ideas, and learn how to take control of our lives.

This imaginative activity is similar to what Einstein did at age 16 when he imagined himself riding along a ray of light to study its properties and resolve problems with Newtonian physics. It is similar to man's invention of culture through language, myth, art, technology, and science—imagining what is not before us. Somewhere two or three million years ago man's ancestors imagined a tree branch detached from the trunk that could be used as a weapon for hunting or self-defense; the one-year-old boy today pictures in his mind the object his mother has just taken from him and hidden behind her back. She can no longer fool him, and he reaches for the toy he cannot see. When David's older brother and sister were sitting in the laundry room one day when he was four or five, they became a little bored looking at the dryer spin the clothes with such monotonous regularity and so they asked themselves, "What would be more fun to look at?" In walked David, and they immediately imagined him as a toy spinning madly with all the clothes. With a little coaxing David climbed into the dryer, his brother set the machine for "fluff dry," and he and his sister sat back and enjoyed the sight of their little brother bouncing about like a tumbling tumble weed. After hearing this story and confirming it with David's mother, I often pictured him staggering out of the machine, very dizzy and singing "How Dry I Am!"

Such imaginativeness, noted Hannah Arendt (1977), is the foundation of thinking itself—being able to visualize what is not present to one's immediate field of viewing or touching or hearing. And so Laura's seemingly wild speculation about who is a part of whose universe isn't so off-the-wall after all. It is an example of her spontaneous mental flexibility, her ability to take a different perspective upon a problem, and to toy with ideas. It is a flexibility that is evident in her physical and vocal playfulness as well. In fact, as shall be noted, David's and Laura's playfulness is a flexible and adaptive response to their environment as evident in their physical, social, emotional, and intellectual activities. Their imaginative thinking is revealed not only through questions and verbal games played on the word "scale," but also through their physical postures and gestures, voice manipulations and imitations, social interactions with friends and adults, and the wide range of emotions they display.

David and Laura are playful individuals who often cause misunderstanding among adults in authority, because of a propensity for having fun and not following the accepted norms of thinking (posing more "serious" questions about the atom) and behaving (being conveniently late when it suits their purposes). Quite often what playful people do is reconstruct a situation in novel and humorous fashion as when Mr. Stump chided a boy for dropping and breaking a large lab thermometer, which one does not shake like a medical thermometer.

"You don't shake *those* down, Scott!"

"I thought you shook all thermometers," Scott answered sheepishly.

"No—you don't shake the thermostat in your house, do you?"

"Yeah, you do!" David piped up smiling broadly. "All you do is get a crane to lift the whole house and shake it *and* the thermostat." Mr. Stump grinned.

By juxtaposing heavy construction equipment with thermostat shaking, David created a vivid image and reassembled the elements of Mr. Stump's problem. Reconstructing the parts of a problem (the "givens" in a situation) involves flexibility of movement within various contexts—physical, social, emotional, and intellectual. Changing and bending the rules of school or volley ball, altering the roles they play in the halls and in the locker room, or varying the meanings of words and common objects like a teacher's bald head are indications of the broad spectrum of behaviors within which these students act. Toying with objects or ideas and imaginatively transforming the visual images we create on canvases of our minds are what playful people do well and what all of us do when we play, think creatively and productively, and take control of our lives.

Where others may see themselves, their feelings, and objects within their environments in more conforming, predictable, static ways, individuals like David and Laura are flexible and fluid enough to change perspectives almost at will:

- One minute they are serious students passing through the halls or listening to a teacher, the next they can be pretending to be Fred Astaire or two cha-cha dancers singing and laughing their cares away.
- One minute a tin can is a tin can, the next it may be a "home for

insects, an abstract art piece, a circular dressing room, or a
bizarre book cover."
- They can imagine what would happen if a fog descended on
  earth so thick that all people could see were each other's feet: "a
  boost for short people, double knit vested socks would be in
  vogue, and nobody would see eye-to-eye on anything" (Torrance, 1966).

These acting and thinking abilities derive from a child's play experiences. Play is characterized by internal control and motivation
in which players create an imaginary world with its own time, setting, rules to follow, and roles to fill. Play is bending reality to one's
own ego, reversing the normal control patterns that exist in the
everyday world—from outer control by others, usually adults, to
inner control by oneself and his or her playmates. Play transcends
the constraints of an immediate situation, transporting us into a
world of timelessness; children can accelerate time by compressing
one week into five minutes of playing "house" or reverse time by
pretending to be two when they are six.

For me, play is a process of transcending above and beyond daily
work routines and roles wherein very often we are doing somebody
else's bidding—a teacher, an employer, or a parent. It is the ability
to pretend to be one's mother or father, to imagine oneself as a
scientist discovering a cure for cancer, as an Antarctic explorer risk-
ing subzero temperatures, or a world famous soccer player—it is
this ability to visualize alternative futures that enables human
beings to strive, to seek, to find a good life, a better life than the one
we lead at present. Without imaginative play humankind would be
forever confined to the present; they would be less than factory
workers who do not raise their eyes above the assembly-line machine they are working on.

It is this facility for transcending the immediate physical, emotional, and intellectual situation, to visualize oneself in a different
time and place, to perceive objects as different from the common
understanding of them (tin cans as book covers), to attach new and
more significant meanings to people and places (the classroom suddenly becomes a motor car speedway)—these play activities result

in learning how to be flexible in changing environments, how to be creative in the arts or in the ways of restructuring our lives, how to prepare for emotionally demanding roles, and how to find new meaning for our lives. Exploring new meanings for ourselves is perhaps the most significant element in play for this is how we change, grow, and continually enrich our lives.

If this is play, what then is playfulness? Throughout my work with these imaginative youngsters, I have relied upon the idea that what we do as children on the playgrounds becomes a part of us as adolescents and adults. The richer our play as children, the more likely we will become playful adolescents and adults. Playfulness can be understood, thanks to my colleague Nina Lieberman (1977), as a personality trait among adolescents, a trait characterized by a sense of humor, manifest joy, and spontaneity in social, physical, and intellectual domains. What impressed me while watching David and Laura will become evident in reading the vignettes about a day in each of their lives. Let me say at the outset that the incidents recorded here all occurred spontaneously, mostly as the result of either David's or Laura's desire to be playful, to take control of a situation, and turn it around for their own purposes. As a result of their many different ways of having fun, they appear to be very flexible in their approach to life—they exercise their ability to transcend immediate social, emotional, physical, or intellectual situations and make something else out of them. This flexibility, I believe, is crucial to becoming healthy adaptable adults who are in control of their lives.

A DAY IN DAVID'S LIFE

David bounded down the hallway between morning classes saying hello to every other boy and girl he passed until he saw one of his close friends on crutches up ahead. Tim, a star soccer player who suffered a fractured ankle during practice, was negotiating the passageway with some difficulty aided though he was by one of his many girlfriends, each as attractive as he was. Sneaking up behind Tim, David grabbed the right crutch in one hand and Timmy around the waist with the other hand—

"Gotcha, you animal!" he shouted catching Timmy completely off guard. What ensued was a game of tug-o-war over the crutch with Timmy struggling desperately to maintain his balance on one foot with the other crutch flaying wildly in the still air like the sword of a swashbuckling pirate.

"Hey! C'mon, Jerk-off! I'm not in the mood for dancin'."

"Oh, yes you are!" retorted the spear carrier who lunged at Timmy with the liberated weapon. Parries and deep thrusts into an unprotected abdomen forced Timmy to bump into passersbys more intent upon being in class before the late bell rang.

"Hey, David! Goddamit! WaddamIsupposadohere?!!" he said laughingly angry and falling near an open locker with the rubber tipped crutch preying at his belly button in smirking conquest. "You wait'll I get my two feets back together again."

Dropping the crutch in mid hallway David suddenly transformed himself into a karate chopping street fighter, high kicking his victim right into the open locker where Tim's slim waist barely fit.

The bell finally rang, and as precipitously as this scenario began, David broke off being Errol Flynn and Kung Fu—"See ya sucker! When I find your other foot I'll turn it into Honeysuckle's lost'n found!" he shouted in a high chuckle at his reference to the principal's burgeoning storehouse of sweat pants, knives, pot accessories, and books that are boring even before opening. Off to history for another session of listening quietly to the facts in Chester Arthur's case.

During history David became thoroughly uninvolved in Chester A. Arthur and slipped away to the Elysian soccer fields of his mind.

"Now if we use Becker on the front line instead of Rogers, maybe we can bust 'em. . . .Here's the ball—atta way Becker! Restrain. . . .Concentrate now. . . .I got him. . . .Get with it. . . .Good ball!!!!"

"Chester Arthur's administration, on the other hand. . ." intoned Mr. Daily as he sat at his lectern hardly varying his position or his voice.

And Dave doodled and wrote his current girl friend's initials on the desk in a variety of combinations together with his own: J.A.. J.T.A., jta. . . ."Why can't her friends understand that I didn't mean it *that* way? They always get in the goddam way. . ." he mused to himself.

"Chester Arthur, of course. . ." was still in the same historical context, right after the assassinated Garfield and just before Grover Cleveland, and Mr. Daily was still discussing, sometimes with himself, the mysteries of the Civil Service reform legislation of 1883.

The cord on the venetian blinds in David's hands became a hangman's noose, a sailor's sheepshank, and ultimately a cowboy's lasso.

"Chester A. Arthur, naturally would have preferred. . ." to have the bell ring as it finally did, and David arose immediately, circled around behind Daily's motionless backside bidding him a cheerful "'afternoon, Mr. Daily" as he usually did, and bolted out the door chumming his way down the stairwell with Banducci. "And of *course* Chester AAAAAAAAAAAAAArthur's service was so civil. . .Oh my God!" he roared, his affected English accent piercing the close walls of another Arthurian dungeon.

The best drummer of the high school band strode into the confusion of setting up music stands, passing out music for the day, and retrieving instruments from their cubby holes in the anteroom, while two parents hustled around collecting moneys for the Giant Crate of Oranges Sale. The Giant Crate of Oranges Sale seems to have been an annual ritual dreamed up by adults (students were less or more interested in it depending upon the proximity of their seats to the director's) in which huge trailer trucks convoyed up from Florida laden with boxes of grapefruits and oranges that were ultimately squeezed into the hands of teachers and students cajoled into buying their vitamin C to support some worthy cause—many were not exactly sure when or where.

To all this confusion, of course, David promptly contributed by seizing an appropriate moment to transform himself Snoopy-style into a behind-the-lines infantryman crawling from his platoon headquarters in the drum section across treacherous enemy territory (so called because it was open to view by Mr. Joe Tarafuccian, the director, who kept an eagle eye upon open spaces between sections lest there be fraternization of some kind thus spoiling the purity of each sound). Within seconds he stealthily came upon the all-girl flute section manned by two neophytes whose playing resembled a kid's first tryouts on a two wheeler—very tentative at best. Unbeknownst to the flutists, David, concealed behind their music stands, was losing his infantry status. Popping up out of the trenches, he became a Punch marionette, shocking Maryann and Susan right out of the struggle to blow out a solid B flat for Mr. Tarafuccian.

"Davie, my God! Ya don't have ta fool around now do ya?!"

Grabbing Susan's ski hat from atop her flute case David improvised a hand puppet and jabbered away with the girls while still on his knees, his puppet hand darting about the music and poking at Susan's chin adoringly.

Mr. Tarafuccian was still struggling with a few awkward notes from the brass section where John Stigliato's chair now was leaning back at least 23½° because John often wanted to be directly parallel to the earth's axis.

"C'mon!! Goose the butterfly!" Tarafuccian yelled, jabbing the air upward with his baton less like Toscanini than a kid giving someone the finger.

"Brasses get your lips up there," he cajoled as Dave pursed up his lips peering over the top of the music stand and tickled Maryann's chin with the ski hat—a bussing bunny rabbit scampering over the fields to its little garden of fresh delicacies.

Back with the snare drums David waited his cue to provide the necessary martial rolls during a Korean folk song. Once completed and with 13 bars of uninterrupted idleness, a glance at Tarafuccian's conducting gyrations propelled David into his own imitation of a maestro's magic, which quickly transformed itself, as the beat slowed, into a gentle Fred Astaire glide across a glitteringly glazed dance floor. With a wave of the hand dumpy Bobby Cartwright, neophyte kettle drummer, momentarily became a Ginger Rogers being pirouetted around Fred's right index finger, which gently floated through the lower jet streams flowing within the music room. From drummer to Toscanini to Astaire all without moving a foot from the pedal of his base drum.

When the bell rang, David was tapping out a rhythm on his knees with a flap of his long, bony elbows and with a quick flight from Tarafuccian's battle weary baton he was out in the social swirl of the corridors once again. Weaving his way down the hall, he bounced from one group of friends to another, like a heated molecule ricocheting off its neighbors.

Just before arriving at the door of the chemistry lab, two hulking football jocks grabbed David around his slim waist and shoulders in a gang tackle and mockingly pummeled him into the wall, where he slowly slipped to the floor hands protecting his ears and eyes.

"Oh, hello wall! and good morning to you too, fellas!" the smile slowly appeared behind his clenched fists. Extricating himself from their vice-like grips, he regained his floating composure and back-pedaled the remaining few steps into chemistry trying to cover his rear flank from another sneak attack.

The bell rang as David crossed the threshold of this world of scientific investigation, and with the circumspection of a comic taking stock of his audience, David instantly realized that Mr. Stump was absent. Closing the door behind him, he strode to center stage, raised his right index finger to his lips commanding silence, and looking to left, center, and right announced, "He's late, folks!" The audience was in the palm of his hand for those five seconds until Stump walked in to a burst of laughter. Checking all his buttons and zippers, he decided it was safe to proceed and went over to his giant lab desk to shuffle some papers prior to commencing class.

David put his books on the desk and in glancing toward the front of the room realized there was another opportunity to be seized. He walked right up to his teacher, took out a pencil from Stump's white smock coat, and pretended to write notes on the massively domed bald head before him while Stump stood there momentarily stunned.

"Hey, whadja do that for?" asked a neighbor when David returned to his seat.

"Instead of looking at the cuff of my shirt during the test, I'll just ask him to come over here and bend down a little," grinned David.

"My god, you're crazy!" laughed his friend.

Settling down to work Mr. Stump introduced a new unit on gasses and pressure. Demonstrating the effects of pressure differentials he filled a beaker full of water and deftly placed a piece of cardboard over the mouth, then inverted the beaker. Students observed that the water did not rush out when Mr. Stump removed his hand from the cardboard.

An explanation of this phenomena ensued that didn't quite satisfy David.

"What if the beaker had had several large bubbles in it?"

Mr. Stump demonstrated and explained.

"What if the beaker were only half full?" David was beginning to smile.

Mr. Stump demonstrated and explained.

"What would happen if you took a dinner plate full of water, turned it upside down over a piece of cardboard, would it stay then?" David was now grinning.

Mr. Stump demonstrated and explained.

"What if you poured all the oceans into the center of the earth and turned it upside down?" David was thoroughly enjoying his little game of mental acrobatics, "and put a giant piece of—"

"O.K., David, we haven't much more time for your imaginings now," and the class laughed on into the next topic.

For a while David lapsed into musings about the film he was making for English and history. "How do you show man's basic traits down through history? What is the most basic characteristic of man, anyway. . .How about greed? . . .always grabbing, taking, out for himself only. . . . How do you portray this to an audience? How do you dramatize a song like "Gimme Dat Ding"?

There were no pat answers to these inner explorations for David had never done anything like this before. He wanted to do something out of the ordinary for this assignment, something people would get a kick out of, and something that would give him some more time on his own—a film!

"What does indigent mean?" asked Carol suddenly, bringing David back to the reality of the English homework she was doing in chemistry.

"Poor," answered Linda in a whisper.

"You don't have to pay taxes," replied David leaning across the aisle staring into her blue eyes as she laughed at the oddity of his answer.

"Shhhhhh" pleaded Sara, the class curve raiser. *"I'm* trying to hear what's going on."

Mr. Stump was rather oblivious to these goings on intent as he was at explaining the intricacies of Boyle's law.

"Oh, c'mon Sarah, what're you afraid of—got teacher phobia—testitis?—got *authorophobia?*" and he laughed at his invention as Mr. Stump drilled away at another explanation.

The bell rang again, and David scurried off to gym, bouncing off three or four more friends on the way. After dressing in baggy blue sweat pants and a red "Kiss Me I'm Left Handed" T-shirt, he strode out onto the floor ready for bear.

"Hey! Killer! How're ya doin'?!"

"Great," David replied as he grabbed a volley ball off the floor and gestured to several chums to gather round for a quick game before attendance.

"Hey, animal, whyn't you get over there," he suggested to even the sides up at three apiece. Just as the teams became even all five players looked to David to make the first serve, as they usually did.

"C'mon, Davie boy! Stab it!"

"Waste it away Dave!" shouted Bryan opposite the net from David as he and his teammates looked up, above the net where the ball would naturally sail. David poised the ball in his left hand and swung his right hand back ready to hit the ball high into the rafters. With his eyes focused above the net and hands at shoulder height ready to spike the ball, Bryan suddenly reeled backwards as the ball was rifled under the net catching him smack on the left knee cap. Surprise! Surprise!

When Bryan awoke to the fact that David had caught them off balance with his unorthodox game plan, he was galloping off to the other end of the gym for attendance.

"Hey, you play by your own rules, dummie?" Bryan shouted still slightly amazed and wishing to drive his playmate into the well-polished floor never to rise and find them with their guard down again.

While all students sat in neat rows to facilitate the recording of attendance, David lay down in the last row and tossed the volley ball up in the air nonchalantly.

"O.K., listen now, ladies and gentlemen," commanded Mr. Davenport, "while I give some of you reluctant learners a few pointers on how to defeat the wall with volley ball skills. The wall,

I think, feels a little cocky today, so we have to be somewhat daring if we're going to be victorious." With two or three volunteers the coach set out to demonstrate how to hit the ball up against the wall with the two-handed open palm shot.

Tommy scooted over to David who sat up straight for a change, and they exchanged pokes in the ribs and shoulder while laughing about their escapade yesterday afternoon with the snowman in Christine's backyard. Christine, a petite sophomore who lived next door to David, had spent Saturday building a curvacious snowman complete with coal eyes, carrot nose, and whisk broom hair. Spying this icy marvel through his back window, David suddenly thought what fun it would be to play around with it. . .to chop it up? (no). . .to run it through with a harpoon? (no). . .to make it disappear (yes!). So when he, Tommy, and Paul were strolling home from the movies Sunday afternoon, they noticed that Chris's parents were having a party.

"Let's make it disappear," proposed Dave.

". . .and reappear somewhere else!" piped in Paul.

So in the late afternoon dusk and darkness, the three swaggering thieves, bundled up in ski parkas in varying stages of disrepair, dug up the snow man behind Chris' house with considerable difficulty. This operation called for a flexible approach, meaning that in addition to their hands, they had to resort to a rusty, frosted crowbar and a broken tricycle wheel found protruding through January's snows. The freezing winds had solidified the snowman's bottom to the ground to such a degree that the best efforts of three intrepid robbers pushing against the lower belly-button resulted in their tumbling down the embankment rolling over each other like kittens fighting over a little ball of snow. Finally, they extricated Mr. Eskimoose, who suddenly found himself being rolled, tugged, and dragged around the backyard.

["Oh, my God! Where are they going to put me? In the driveway?. . .by the doghouse?. . .on the sidewalk?" mused Mr. Eskimoose in some despair.]

"C'mon, men, right up here on the porch so's old Mr. Boston will fall right over it," laughed David.

" 'Oh, you look so pale, my dear,' " chimed in Paul in an alcoholic falsetto voice. 'You must step inside before you catch a hangover. . .' "

At story's end David finally had to challenge the wall, and this day, like many others, he lost.

Today there was no art class and, consequently, no opportunity to work at one of the four water color assignments staring him in the face. This was good, because David would really rather have spent the time drawing the Cosmic Muffin or adding to his collection of stories, maps, cartoons, and sketches depicting The Land of Whoopie, a territory comprised of the Nattily Wood, the Mystical Volcano of Heineken, The Far Freakin' Forest, and The Land of Peace, Love, Harmony, Brotherhood, and Hard Liquor (see Figure 1). Whoopie was in reality "a state of mind," an escape into an adolescent's natural playfulness and imaginative musings. In David's mind it was often conceived as an escape from the threat of The God of the Five Paragraph Expository Essay and his dastardly red marking pencil, a god to whom everybody from kindergarten on up seemed to pay increasing reverence.

Later in the day in journalism, David and Pete were being interviewed by Debbie for an article she was writing for *High Tide*, the school newspaper.

"C'mon, you clowns—"

"I'm tellin ya truly, Debbie," Dave smiled, enunciating in one of his easily affected imitative voices—that of a lazy cowpuncher. "The *boys'* locker room has Valet Towel and Shower Service. We have a guy who personally delivers you a towel as soon as you step out of the shower—"

"You're kidding! Aren't you!?"

"No," said Pete. "He's reponsible for our foot baths also—little individual puddles we soak our feets in. . . ."

CLANG. . .CLANG. . .CLANG

"Oh, goddamit, not another one!"

The fire alarm interrupted this immensely incisive interview, and David and Pete flashed out of room 225 and down the hall in two seconds. Half way down the stairs, the announcement came to disregard the alarm and proceed back to classes.

The two locker room *mavens* decided to disregard the official dic-

Atheletic Archepalago

ISLAND OF JØK

FLEX INLET

GERITÖL

BAY OF BENGE

THE EVELYN WOOD

THE STRAITS OF

Yaght Docks

Point of No Return

Penninsula of Nikon Zöom and Hasselblad

LAND OF PEACE, LOVE, HARMONY, BROTHERHOOD AND HARD LIQUOR

LITTLE JOE LINGUINI'S PIZZA PARLOUR

Stage Band Five City

Dipthong Delta

LEAST BILGE

RABID RIDGEWOODITES

WHOOPIE (G.M.A.)

ROYAL B

Oboe I

BAY OF MOTOBÉCANE

MESCALINE INLET

LESSER BILGE

THE KNEEHILLS OF BILGE

Revelation Ridge

TOWN OF MINOR BLUES

VALVEOIL SPRING

(Inferior Int

VER

THE SOFT MOOR

GREATER BILGE

Minnisoda Flats

THE DRĀNO MOUNTAINS

LAND OF UNGUENTINE

THE RUDY VALLEY

THE D

CITY OF RON

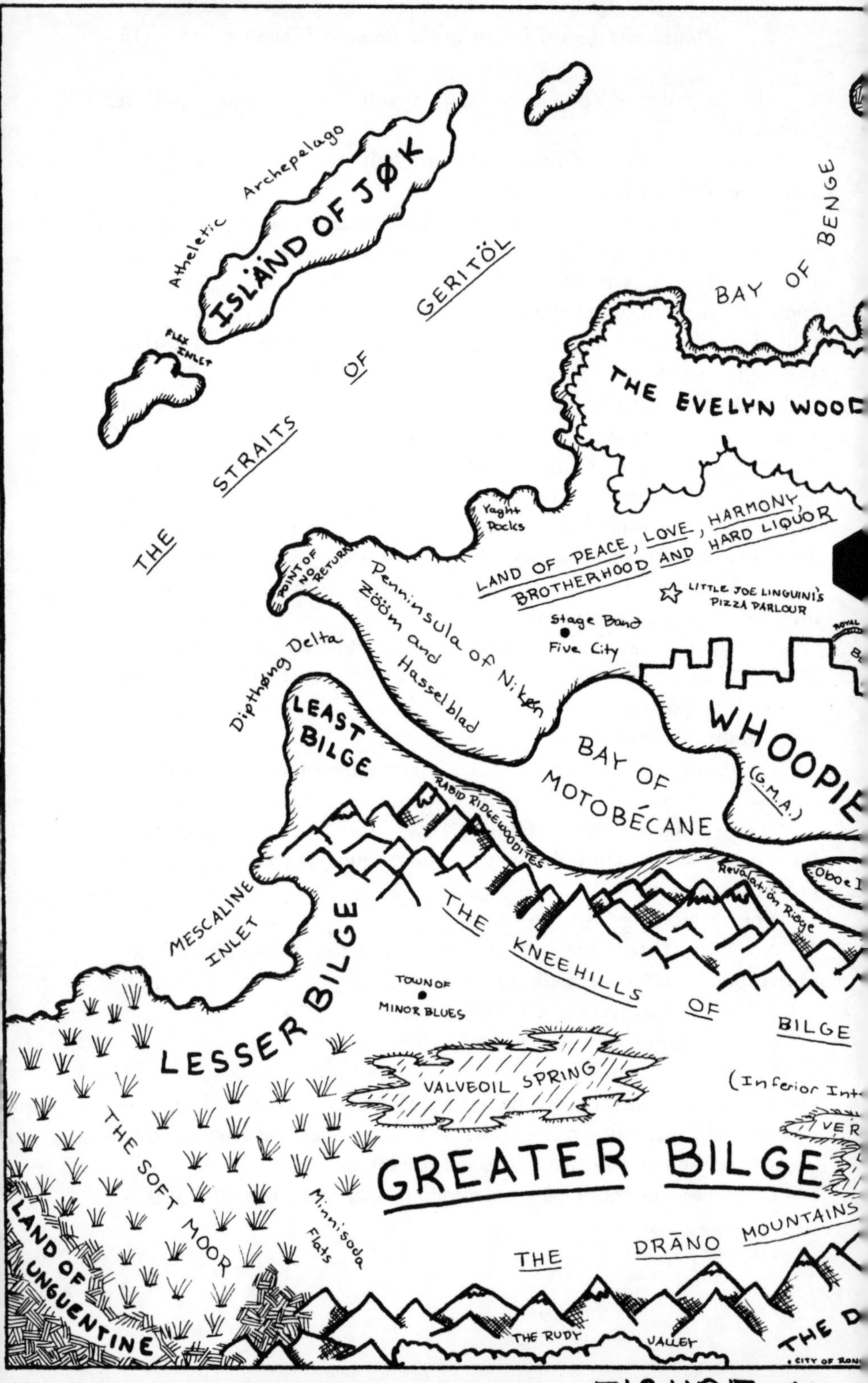

FIGURE 1

Epsilon Boötes

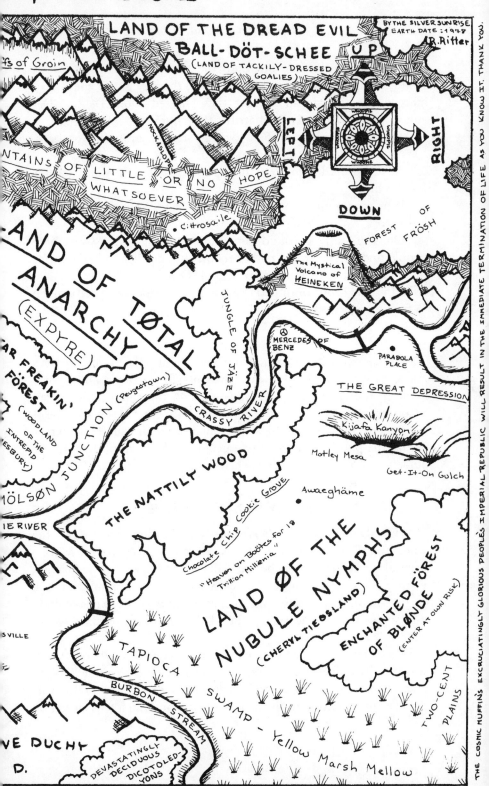

LAND OF THE DREAD EVIL BALL-DÖT-SCHEE (LAND OF TACKILY-DRESSED GOALIES)

...fs of Groin

...NTAINS OF LITTLE OR NO HOPE WHATSOEVER

• Citrosaile

UP

LEFT RIGHT

WHOOPS WHOOPS WHOOPS WHOOPS

DOWN

FOREST OF FRÖSH

The Mystical Volcano of HEINEKEN

BY THE SILVER SUNRISE EARTH DATE : 1978 J.R.Ritter

LAND OF TOTAL ANARCHY (EXPYRE)

...AR FREAKIN' FÖREST ("WOODLAND OF THE INTREPID ...ESBURY)

...MÖLSØN JUNCTION (Peugeotown)

...IE RIVER

JUNGLE OF JÄZZ

CRASSY RIVER

MERCEDES OF BENZ

PARABOLA PLACE

THE GREAT DEPRESSION

Kijafa Kanyon

Motley Mesa

Get-It-On Gulch

THE NATTILY WOOD

Chocolate Chip Cookie Grove

"Heaven on Boötes for 18 Trillion Millenia"

• Awaeghäme

...SVILLE

...VE DUCHY

D.

TAPIOCA

BURBON STREAM

DEVASTATINGLY DECIDUOUS DICOTOLED-YONS

LAND ØF THE NUBULE NYMPHS (CHERYL TIEØSLAND)

SWAMP - Yellow Marsh Mellow

ENCHANTED FÖREST OF BLØNDE (ENTER AT OWN RISK)

TWO-CENT PLAINS

tum and instead strode out onto the school's front yard (or its "main campus" as adults like to call it, thereby giving the school more of a collegiate air). There they chatted about Debbie, Desinex, and R. Donovan Podiatribe, the "humongous" footman.

After several minutes Pete became restive or guilty or both. "Well, I'm gonna go back; you comin'?"

"Naw, I think I'll go up to the typing room and finish my outline for the film."

"Why you gonna do that?" queried Pete. "Seems like such a lotta work."

"Oh, you know, gotta do something different, O.K.? Can't bore people and myself with another report; besides it's a challenge for me. . . .I'll catch ya later, after school, O.K.?"

With this David continued to arrange the school day pretty much to fit his own needs.

Before looking in on Laura's day you might reflect upon the boys and girls you have known who are as playful as David and Laura, for even though they are composites and, therefore, fictionalized accounts, all the events noted here have happened in school. One of my purposes in creating these personalities is for each of us to recognize the playful aspects of real people we know and, then, to ask ourselves of what value are such ways of behaving.

A DAY IN LAURA'S LIFE

While David and Pete were busily discussing how to pull the wool over Debbie's innocent eyes, Laura and her friend Margie were also outside during the fire drill concocting a surprise for their history class the next day. The occasion was the annual yearbook picture-taking ceremony, and such an event was not to pass calmly and serenely as Uncle Harry, their beloved history teacher, would wish.

When class convened the next morning at 8:03 or :04 or :05—it was usually different every morning because Harry's students were always so busy shooting the breeze with each other—no one was paying any attention to the room's only door, which was closed by now. All of a sudden through the door bounded two medium-sized gorillas yelping in high squeaky voices and jumping up and down together like two pieces of hot popping corn.

"Call media!" shouted Ken over the jungle noises. "We have a *Planet of the Apes* rerun!" Everybody watched with mixed feelings of amusement, awe, or indifference.

The gorillas' fangs were short and white, and little red tongues stuck out ever so slightly from the mouths, which were surrounded by dark brown greasy hair. These diminutive australopithecines then began to bounce about the horseshoe shaped desk arrangement, plucking imaginary bananas from behind peoples' ears, tapping them on the head, and rustling up papers on a few desks as if looking for the last few berries for the day's dinner.

"Get Darwin on the phone!" yelled Paula. "The missing link's right here!"

"Let's have another trial," added Ken as he wrestled briefly with one of the over-sized chimps. "We got the monkeys to make the case!" The gorillas had worked their way back to Harry's desk when shy, sensitive Susan unexpectedly walked into the midst of the two jumping, screeching creatures.

"Oh, my God!" she gasped, clutching her throat like Faye Wray confronting a snarling King Kong. Thinking she'd made a mistake, she tried to leave but was soon surrounded and gently pummeled like an entrapped beast of prey being subjected to a primitive ritual dance before slaughter. "I'm too young to die!" shrieked Susan as she pulled herself away and found her seat very quickly.

The furor died down, and the unmasking of the gorillas revealed the laughing and slightly perspiring faces of Laura and Margie.

"I should have known you had something to do with this Laura," laughed Harry as he attempted to restore some semblance of order. But his picking up the gorilla's head and almost putting it on himself didn't help matters much.

"Go, Harry!" rang out shouts of encouragement.

"O.K., let me have your attention please," asked Harry as he attempted to find a way to bridge the gap from the shrinking forests of the African savannah two million years ago to the desirability of living in a Marxist state.

Once out of costume Laura did settle down to listening to the class discussion while occasionally playing a game of tic-tac-toe on the back of her notebook with Paul or taking brief glances at her math homework. She and Margie still laughed over their escapade, over the effectiveness of their surprise.

Laura is a good "screener;" like David, she can screen in or out classroom conversations according to their significance for her. Consequently, while looking totally preoccupied or bored in her doodling or idle chit chat with Paul, she suddenly sat bolt upright in her chair. "How can you say that?" she exclaimed, pointing a prosecutorial finger at Harry in heated courtroom style.

"You guys are missing a point here! If you brought in people from Mars who haven't had our experience, you could have a class-less society, but *we* can't forget our class system." Her voice rose in a slightly pleading tone, "Only if we grew up on another planet. . . ."

"Laura," interrupted Harry. "All you have to do is kill a few capitalists, and we'll have the classless society right here in the United States." Harry loved the give and take of a good goading session such as this, where he got to play a different role just as Laura had in her costume.

"We've been mind-washed," she continued a little more composed but not more convincing to her friends. "Only if you put us in a little container and turn on the laser beam, will you get rid of these human qualities."

Margie leaned over with a grin and whispered, "Outta sight, kid!"

At the bell Laura lingered longer than David might to talk with Uncle Harry and perhaps offer yet another challenge to him: "You're afraid to drive with me to the class party tomorrow night aren't you? That's why you're going with a junior—of all things!"

Harry laughed, denied any apprehension about driving with Laura in her little VW, and proceeded to reassure one of his best students: "Laura, I never knew what beauty could reside in such a beast." They both laughed and parted.

Out the door and down the halls toward Spanish. En route Laura said "Hi" to ten or twelve friends, boys and girls from different social groups within the school from the gear heads to the rah-rahs, from the jocks, male and female, to the disco dancers.

The bell rang and Laura was invariably somewhere other than in her assigned seat. When she appeared at the door sometimes two or three minutes late, her smiling effervescence eased her way past the teacher, Mrs. Hernandez.

Laura's way of settling down to business was first to glance over at "Juanita" as Mrs. Hernandez called Jean and to whisper messages about last night's telephone conversation with Walter, or about the poem she had just written for her grandfather's birthday, or the poem she wrote about an unrequited love.

Eventually the class was organized into small groups with the intention of writing a brief summary of chapter four in the short novel they were reading.

Laura assumed a leadership role in asking for a secretary and then proceeded to offer a variety of suggestions for wording the summary: "Perhaps we could say. . . . What if we worded it this way. . .? Suppose we change that to mean. . .? It might be better this way. . . ." With each suggestion her hands moved to various parts of her face: on her chin, right hand on left cheek, both behind her ears combing her light brown hair back into a pony tail, one upon a temple, two upon her eyes.

Laura's hands mirrored every new idea or suggestion she offered the group: each new physical position reflected her mentally toying with verbs, nouns, and adjectives on the grammatical jungle gym of her mind. The problem of what to say and how to say it challenged her to a game of mental acrobatics, and her body manifested the spontaneity and flexibility of her thinking.

Once everybody had approved the final version, Laura and her committee members returned to their original seats, and as soon as Jean's group was also finished, the two of them took up where they had left off:

". . .and we went to the Torremolinos last night for dinner," her smile suddenly broke into laughter as she continued, "and there were Spaniards on our left and right speaking *so* beautifully!" At the thought of the festivities her whole body perked and bubbled like a little coffee pot. ". . .and the tostados and mole con pollo. . ." and her laughter bubbled forth as if from a spring of natural effervescence deep within her. She was now like an actress whose imagination easily conjured up concrete images of happy experiences with people and with sights and sounds and tastes—and these images, carefully selected, most often evoked sensations of joy and the excitement of life. It was perhaps the vividness of her emotional recall that caused an acquaintance to note, while Laura was trying on ski boots on her Lake Placid camping trip, that "Laura sure is high on life, isn't she?"

After Spanish Laura headed to the library to work, or more accurately, to talk with her friends. One might see her bouncing from one conversation to another, standing with Pauline near the door whispering about their camping trip during which Laura almost drove the family van deep into the minus thirty degree temperatures of the frozen Adirondacks without any antifreeze in the radiator.

"Can you imagine that! No antifreeze!" she flung her hands up in despair. "If Ken hadn't said something when we were at the last gas station before Lake Placid, whaddya suppose woulda happened?" she laughed almost too loudly for the librarian, who pointed her pencil menacingly in the girls' direction.

"You might've had a good time, I bet; but your Dad would've had a *cow* over it."

Laura's absentmindedness was as evident as that of the professor who brings the wrong lecture notes to his class. Driving down the highway en route to their outdoor lean-tos during the previous week, she had chattered on about six different subjects almost simultaneously, usually managing to keep at least *one* hand on the wheel but hardly noticing that she was heading precisely for the left front fender of a Cadillac Eldorado whose body stuck halfway out into the road. Taking a micro-second from the spinning of tales short and tall, she noticed the obtruding fender with about five feet to spare and swerved around it.

"My God! Laura!"

"Sorry, boys and girls!" she chuckled as if she'd only spilled a little coffee or tea on the table.

Back in the library, Laura realized there was a little work to be done so she found a table and opened her book only to be interrupted by Janet who came bouncing over like a little rabbit with her fingers sticking up behind her ears.

"Hi! Whatcha doin'?" Janet asked sitting down across the table, resting her chin on top of her chemistry text.

"A little history for the test next period—we seem to have a test twice a week!" she replied with some desperation and much disinterest.

"Did you see Deirdre? She's a back from Scandinavia—I had dinner with her last night, and she taught me some Swedish."

"What?"

Yoürk knarc!" Janet said hardly able to contain her laughter. "Know what it means? 'I take drugs!' "

"Ahhh, *'Estoy tomando drogas!'* "Laura laughed so loudly that the librarian put her book cards down and again pointed that pencil at her offensively.

"Estás tomando drogas?" shot back Janet as they both muffled their giggles in their hands lest their exit be sooner and more unwilling than anticipated.

Safely enduring study period without forcible ejection, Laura dropped in on the cafeteria, where students sit at well-designed alcoves surrounded by low partitions fashioned out of beautifully stained white pine. In the center of the space is a three-step high island, carpeted with more alcoves for even greater privacy. Laura visited with friends on the island for a while and then retired to her favorite spot over in the corner on ground level.

"Hey Lisa. Seen Mary Beth recently?"

Laura sat down at Lisa's table, which was covered with an algebra II book, a half empty carton of milk with the metric tables printed neatly on each side so one could memorize the equivalents of the inch and foot between gulps, and a half-eaten hamburger bun.

"No, I haven't—last time was in gym this morning."

Laura was hungry but didn't feel like idling herself on the food line just yet, so she stared at the hamburger bun sitting on a piece of Saran Wrap. The more she stared at it, the more it seemed unlike something one ate and more like a partial human torso. She picked it up, played around with it in her hands for a moment.

"Oh, put that down! That's gross, Laura! Somebody just left it here—gross me out!" Lisa said scrinching up her nose at the left-over food.

"It's kinda cute in a funny way," Laura replied, placing it on the red formica table top and putting two abandoned straw wrappers beneath it for legs. Lisa suddenly became a little more interested now that the two of them were looking at the hamburger bun *as if* it were a human body; she quickly found some raisins for eyes and a piece of napkin for a head.

"Let's make her a bikini," said Laura with a laugh as she went over to another table to recover bits of red tin foil, tore it up into two pieces and decked her little doll out in a revealing Riviera outfit. The once and former hamburger bun had been transformed in the middle of the dining table into a senorita making it on the hot Mediterranean sands.

"You goonin' around again Laura?" asked Betsy as she sat down next to Lisa.

"Yep," beamed Laura, "just like my daddy taught me. Remember all those crazy toys he used to bring home? Where would I be today? How's your brother, Bets?"

"Oh, just great! He's goin' through hazing right now. Ya know what he had to do? Swallow a goldfish!"

"Gross!" shrieked Laura puckering up her mouth and nose as if tasting pure Tabasco for the first time. "What a taste! I couldn't *stand* it—never—drive me mental in a minute. . . .Oh, God, how'd you get it out of there—ya know—if you just couldn't stand to let it make the round trip?"

"Whatta mind, Laura!" Betsy roared leaning back in her chair and placing her feet up on the table's edge. "Let's see, you could cut open the stomach—"

"Swallow a fish hook with a worm on the end," added Lisa.

"No, no, I got it!" Laura leaned forward with excitement almost crushing Riviera Rita and her red bikini. "Float it out by swallowing three gallons of Kool Aid!"

Everybody loved that solution, but the bell rang, and there wasn't much time to sit around and enjoy it.

"See you guys!" smiled Laura as she picked up her books and

headed for humanities just up the first floor hallway from the "cafe" as everybody called it. She was only 30 seconds late for the first reel of *Citizen Kane,* but the lights had already been dimmed and with some difficulty she found her seat down in the first row of the amphitheater-shaped room. Watching Orson Welles slowly build his empire was usually captivating, yet if you've seen him do it before, you allow your playful mind to entertain possibilities other than sitting there with your eyes riveted upon him at one end of his mile-long dining room table in his Hearst-like mansion. Sitting became boring, and Laura suddenly plopped down on the classroom floor and started to crawl infantry-style back up the sloping floor toward her friend Sam, who sat in the fifth row. With the movie lights flickering above like so many bombs bursting in air, Laura crawled among the unsuspecting feet.

"Oops! Pardon!" she whispered in her affected Spanish accent, sounding much like Mel Blanc on the Jack Benny radio show. Up to the third row and still undetected by the teacher who, fortunately, sat very close to the projector way up in the back of the room, Laura's hand groped for the next step and found upon it the tell-tale pair of torn Adidas running shoes worn to such a frazzle that the big toe nearly rested on the floor rather than on the cushion of protective and padded rubber.

"My god! What—? Who—?" Laura was gently pinching Sam's big toe as a calling card. She raised herself up into the empty seat, smiling, with a little dirt on her brown corduroy jeans.

"Just thought I'd come by to say hello. Surprised?"

Sam laughed, "At first I thought the rats were coming to get us."

"Oh, thanks a lot!" Laura sighed as she settled into her seat and began to kibbitz with Sam as Citizen Kane built his edifice to the human ego.

At the bell Laura blinked her eyes a few times to get used to the light, while those around her blinked just at the sight of her sitting in someone else's seat for a change.

"How'd you get there, Laura?" Marie asked in amazement probably because there was a certain predictability to everything in this class.

"She made like Castro in the jungle," chuckled Sam as they left the amphitheater and Laura said goodbye.

Quickstepping off to creative writing Laura had not gone far before she ran into Margie again at the intersection of two hallways, which with students milling about between bells made it much like Times Square during rush hour. At the sight of one another Margie and Laura spontaneously burst into a song and dance routine: "Cha cha cha. . .Saturday night. . .Kansas City. . ." and onrushers to class were only mildly aware that two dance hall dollies were doing it up and causing a minor traffic jam.

"I was just thinking about that Saturday night, Margie! Isn't that amazing!"

"I know," Margie laughed as she settled into a one-step. "God, how fantastic that music is," and her breathing became a little more relaxed and gently rhythmic. That "Saturday night" had been an improvisational extravaganza at Laura's house where the two high steppers had transformed a dance tune heard on the radio into their own combination of cha cha and disco with a little TV variety hour dashed in like a pinch of salt to a cake mix.

Creative writing was just around the corner, and Laura breezed in—late again—waved at Mrs. Simmons who, in a slight fit of exasperation, decided to wave back with a resigned smile. "What does one do with such a child?" she asked herself. The classroom was arranged in that horseshoe formation so prevalent at Laura's school, a nice relaxed arrangement where teachers could establish very close contact with each student if that was desirable. Laura sat right at the center of the horseshoe opposite the teacher's desk, a spot so chosen that should the fancy strike she could be the focus of attention—center stage as it were.

While Mrs. Simmons was structuring the class's writing time, Laura was huddled with Stacy whispering *sotto voce* about her little family of four girls she tended every Monday and Wednesday afternoons. "Yesterday I was reading the kids this story, and they just loved it! I'd love to write one like that—"

"Laura? Are you with us?" asked Mrs. Simmons peering over her steel rimmed glasses resting on the end of her nose.

"Sorry," replied the story teller in a slight singsong voice. When directions were completed, everybody more or less started working, although for some students it was an opportunity to crowd over by the windows and play the old game of "catching the rays" pouring into the room on the first day of March. Amidst the plants on the windowsill eventually two boys and a girl were writing and reclining.

"William, would you get your big toe out of my African violets please? Thank you." Mrs. Simmons was a plant parent, and the room received as much oxygen from her plants as from the fresh air blowing in through the windows.

"Can we go outside today, Mrs. Simmons?" asked Laura interrupting the concentration of those who had commenced the assignment and of those who were concentrating on their own daydreams.

"Maybe tomorrow, Laura."

"Maybe we can go up on the roof?" Laura chimed in with a broad smile thinking she had wrung a concession from Mrs. Simmons, who was just as anxious to leave the confines of room 228.

Laura did start to work on her story. It was hard for her to concentrate in such "writing labs" with everybody else present, but she managed five lines, thought they were terrible, and crumpled up three pieces of paper at once.

"Ayyy, this'll drive me mental!" she said to Stacy. Laura sat there rolling the paper into tighter and tighter little balls thinking of how different her story was from the one she read to the Parker children. "Christine wouldn't be able to even *follow* this thing," she whispered loudly in desperation; "wouldn't find this opening interesting at all!" With the papers in her hand Laura looked across the room at the wastebasket sitting by Mrs. Simmons' desk: "Dump these scraps and start over," she said to herself. Like an actress with the option of entering stage left or right, she could go either way around the horseshoe. But she suddenly stood up and climbed upon the chair, then the desk, paused for a microsecond as if catching the audience's attention and leapt to the floor arms outstretched landing perfectly on center stage. In five seconds she strode to the wastebasket, deposited the papers, pivoted on her left heel, aimed straight for the leaping ledge and made for it without so much as a "how do you do?" to Mrs. Simmons who, like some of the others, was not quite certain whether or not last night's full moon had triggered the "weird" switch in Laura's brain.

At the bell the short story had a beginning, which Laura could tolerate for now, but she didn't linger to discuss it with Mrs. Simmons or Tracy. The day was too beautiful to do anything but go outdoors during gym and run for two miles or so. "Call me, tonight, Stacy O.K.?" she smiled ebulliently and dashed downstairs to the locker room where she changed in ten minutes, had her attendance taken, and breezed off onto the roads leading away from the high school.

Many people consider running the ultimate in boring sports, but not Laura. For her running was an opportunity to clear her mind of all the school work, all the entangling facts that were hurled, tossed lightly, or banked in on a curve toward her memory bins. It was a release from the pressure to receive and reproduce someone *else's* thinking—it was a time to be totally free and in control to think and create her own thoughts. Unlike most of her classes, while running Laura decided the rules of the game, she posed the questions, she created the toys to be played with. Indeed, she selected the game to be played, not somebody else. Running was not boring—it was playing and, therefore, liberating and lots of fun.

The sidewalks of town were clear leaving Laura the freedom to concentrate upon her own thoughts. She wondered what Andre in *War and Peace* felt lying on the battleground looking up at the stars, jumped to a scene of a boy riding a magic unicorn through space in her favorite children's story and wondered how to fit it into her term paper for Uncle Harry on children's literature, played school with Christine allowing her to be the teacher and played her game with Harry called "What Can I Think of That *You* Haven't Thought of"—"Did the ancient Greeks eat ice cream? Do the Chinese have telephones? Tell me what you know Harry; let's see if I can open a door within *your* mind also."

Rounding a bend in a part of town she'd never been to before, Laura noticed the distant hill known as Camelback and wondered why people always called it that. It looked very different from her vantage point, perhaps more like a turtle.

Running wasn't boring—it gave her a new perspective on herself and the problems she thought were meaningful.

REVIEW

The playfulness of David and Laura can now be discussed by addressing two questions:

1. What do these playful actions reveal about their development as adolescents?
2. Of what significance might playfulness be for the educational environments educators design for or with their students?

These two questions will frame the discussion in subsequent chapters of the potential meaningfulness of David's and Laura's imaginative behavior and will, hopefully, disclose some of the possibilities of play within classrooms. Since playfulness reflects spontaneity and flexibility within physical, emotional, social, and cognitive areas, I will discuss them in that order.

Physical Playfulness

David's physical horseplay with friends reflects a spontaneous interaction characteristic of playful people. In clowning around with a crutch, David was having fun in a form often noticed with adolescent boys. A familiar greeting for boys is a rather hard punch in the arm, grabbing someone around the neck wrestling fashion, or sneaking up behind a friend and clamping a hammer lock on him while he's dressing in the locker room. Often such overtures, accompanied by verbal put downs such as "Weasel!", "Faggot!" or "Hey, you animal!" result in rolling, punching, and banging around the hallways or gym—a dynamic duo of laughter and raucous joy just as evident in younger children's games of tag or ring-around-the-rosie.

Laura's physical playfulness includes poking and gently punching friends, usually girls, in classrooms. Once in a while I have observed her sneak up on some unsuspecting boy standing idly by the cafeteria door daydreaming and snap, "Wake up!" pointing a menacing finger, witch like, at his belly and then, in a flash run off, laughing at having caught another victim by surprise.

More often, however, Laura is much like an actress using her voice as an instrument of imitation in Spanish, British, or Mel Blanc-style. She whipped off such imitations at the drop of a hat while driving to Lake Placid, relaxing with girl and boy friends, or while playing with the children she baby-sits for. Doing a soft shoe routine or a "Cha cha. . .Saturday Night" is more typical of her improvisational style than David's aggressive horseplay. Thus, there may be more novelty in Laura's clowning than in David's. However, both David and Laura transform themselves from students to fighters and dancers. And the joy of this transcendence, noted Nina Lieberman (1977) "may also be rooted in a sense of mastery. . .it indicates an ability of restructuring materials into a fantasy context" (p. 81). David feels this mastery not only in his horseplay, but in heading a soccer ball away from his goal; Laura feels it when she is out running. It is important to note further, I think, that there does not appear to be a clearly delineated separation between David's physical clowning with a crutch and Laura's less aggressive soft shoe routines: each can do both, and this is a further indication of their flexibility.

Actors studying their craft learn how to express physically feelings of joy, pain, or sadness; they show through gesture and expression the emotions rather than saying, "Oh, I have this horrible stomach ache!" The emotions David and Laura reflect in their clowning seem to be primarily ones of affection for others with displeasure expressed occasionally. Rather than sit in a classroom or walk down the corridors holding in their feelings, these youngsters act them out when the need arises, and this produces pleasure. As I watched them, I often wondered if David and Laura were growing up to be adults who could express a broader range of emotions than other people—whether their physical playfulness was endowing them with the ability to play many more emotional roles on the stage of life from a despairing Macbeth to an idealistic Biff.

And, finally, the different roles David and Laura enact through their imitativeness reflect for them a certain emotional identification with other roles, oftentimes those of adults. These attachments to people who are highly regarded form part of the adolescent's constellation of role models. Freud perceived such identifications as the essence of children's dramatic playing of house, that is, through imitation we express our wish to grow up. Erikson suggests that adolescents are re-evaluating these childhood identifications in the process of restructuring their own identities. This is not to say, of course, that David's playing a karate expert or Laura's playing a disco dancer means these roles represent career selections for them; I think it only means that whomever one chooses to imitate reflects an emotional attachment, strong or weak, and that these imitations may represent some experimentation with different ways of expressing feelings.

In *Portrait of the Artist as a Young Man* (Joyce, 1956) Stephen Dedalus breaks loose from the constraints of family, Church, and Ireland and sets forth upon a new career as an artist who will "recreate life out of life." We are, in a sense, artists when we rise above the limitations of the moment to recreate ourselves through physical motions and gestures, a self-transformation of imagining ourselves in new roles.

Social Fluidity

The social playfulness of David and Laura is evident in their being able to interact with a variety of people rather spontaneously. They manifest a social fluidity and flexibility evidenced in their bouncing from group to group as they navigate the school's corridors.

Other people perceive David as one who is not only exciting, funny, and an extrovert, but one who is sensitive to the needs and feelings of other people. Girls often note his empathic understanding of friends' problems. David reaches out to boys and girls who are lonely by extending a comforting greeting or by noticing something complimentary about their appearance. His friends note that he will say hello to and engage in conversation with strangers behind checkout counters, salespeople in stores, and others not known to him. In other words, David is very open to a variety of people, and his flexibility often leads to very challenging situations. For example, he once hitchhiked through unknown New England territory and slept in a stranger's barn with about twenty steaming cows during the dead of winter after accepting rides from many people of widely diversified backgrounds.

Laura knows members of the different social groups in school: the gear heads, who work on cars, the preppies, the jocks, the curve raisers. She can be as comfortable hosting the Spanish Club's international dinner and joking with Mr. Honeysuckle, the principal, about how to make a Mexican dish of chocolate chicken, as she is helping Diane, one of the disco dancers, prepare steak and green beans in a lean-to at 20 degrees below zero.

This adaptability may further reflect the social role-playing Erikson (1974) asserts is a key process in adolescents. An animated TV cartoon of his eight stages of human development dramatized adolescence by showing several youngsters entering an amusement park with the voice coaxing:

> Find yourself—you'll have the thrill of your life cycle. You can be a dreamer—you can be a leader—you can be *anything*. See yourself the way you want to be in the mirror of tomorrow. Want to be powerful? Sure you do! Want to be loved? Everybody does! The roles of passion—the roles of power. . . .Play them all! You'll find your own true self—your very own identity. I dare you, friends! Hurry, Hurry, Hurry. That's it! . . .Take a Chance! (Hubley, 1976)

If David and Laura are finding their own true selves, they may be doing it, in part at least, through their physical and social playfulness. By moving within several different groups, they may be experimenting with different role identifications as Erikson suggests, a process that results in evolving different identities throughout life's several seasons.[1]

The key to their adaptability, I think, is a heightened sense of empathy. Martin Buber (1965) asserted that true dialogue between individuals requires that both "imagine the real" world of the other person, a process akin to empathizing. David and Laura can imagine what it's like to be in the other person's shoes; in fact, Laura seems to deal with interpersonal problems quite often by asking, "Well, how would *you* feel if you were so-and-so?" People without the ability to imagine themselves playing another role are not going to be very open to the differences between social groups within schools or communities. People who do "imagine the real" world of others tend also to be able to relate more closely to other age groups; both David and Laura show a marked ability to relate to and play with children. David teaches them soccer in his front yard any afternoon they're around, and they usually are there because he knows how they think and play. Laura is enamored of children's literature and spends two days a week caring for four younger girls down the street—cooking, playing, helping with homework, and washing hair.

Similarly, what David and Laura admire about some of their teachers is their ability to imagine the real world of their students. Time and again both have told me about teachers who remembered what being a student in high school was like and communicated that well. Not only does Uncle Harry tolerate Laura's pretending to be a gorilla and allow himself to be challenged repeatedly through her game of "What can I think of?" but it is often his practice to return test papers with little cartoons drawn on the last page, which reflect some of the student's main ideas as well as his own comments. It's no wonder that there has been in their school an Uncle Harry Admiration Association for almost twenty years.

Social playfulness, then, means flexibility and fluidity among different peer groups as well as different age groups, and a major determinant in such movement and interaction is the imagination.

Cognitive Restructuring

When David asked his chemistry teacher, "What if I filled a plate full of water, would the water–air pressure experiment work?" and when Laura imagines being zapped by a laser beam to rid her of class consciousness, they are both playing with ideas, allowing ideas, as Laura said, to "roll around in your head." Toying with images is what Bronowski called imagination and what Einstein said was his first step in productive thinking.

David's seeing his teacher's bald head as a place for crib notes and Laura's playing a game of motorboat with a friend's shoe laces (place feet on lap, hold laces, and, while making the sound of an outboard revving up, pull the laces apart) are examples of perceiving objects from different perspectives. This ability is what Torrance and others call ideational flexibility, being able to see a problem from several different angles. Such flexibility is critical to the creative process, because "to see the world in grain of sand," one must maintain an openness to the world and its mysteries, an openness to novel perspectives and viewpoints. For the painter Corot, the key to a good landscape was knowing where to sit.

When in Laura's history class Uncle Harry was discussing the Platt Amendment to the Cuban Constitution, one student said it was "presumptuous of the United States to include a provision" for intervening in their internal affairs. "Seems as if this put us in a position of playing God," she added.

"What's wrong with that?" Laura shot back in a high pitched voice to the amazement of some students. "You're taking the view that the United States was doing the wrong thing—there might have been people who felt they were carrying the white man's burden down to the Cubans." In taking an unpopular position on this question Laura was "rethinking" the past according to historian John Lukacs (Mee, 1976), a playful process that shall be discussed in greater detail in chapter II.

Another example of playing with ideas and attaining an entirely new perspective upon a problem occurred when I asked Laura, "What would happen if atoms were inhabited by thinking beings?" Her replies flowed in this manner, "out of a fog" as she said:

It would start a humane movement for those poor little creatures. . .convince us of the probability of people in outer space. . .they'd be too small to domesticate. . .open up a new field for science. . .people living inside people. . .the earth could then be a big atom in a huge creature. . . .

It was the last thought that struck me as so significant, not only because it represented a high level of abstract thinking (Piaget's formal operations), which can draw conclusions from hypothetical (and, at times, impossible) premises, but also because I have heard other people posing that very question "What if our earth is but a single atom within a giant creature?" As will be noted in chapter IV, how teachers respond to such a question tells much about how they value "combinatory play with ideas," as Einstein called it.

Play is evident, of course, in daydreams. David's daydreams reveal spontaneous recombinations of elements in mentally reshuffling players and their actions on a soccer field or in allowing a history teacher's mention of the location of the Hamilton-Burr duel to trigger a spate of visual images associated with that spot in New Jersey and concluding with the thought question "What would the Manhattan skyline have looked like from Jersey back in 1804?"

Daydreams are the adolescent form of play *par excellence,* the internalized form of child's play. It is a form of visual self-projection into the personal, social, vocational, and recreational roles they do and might play in the future. It can be useful for problem solving of an immediate and practical nature—an opportunity to figure out how to ensure that a girl who's following you around doesn't become too much of a domineering mother-type, or what to do during the break—to go to the ladies room and comb your hair or to go see your boyfriend, then to the ladies room.

Jerome Singer (1976) discovered a relation between the extent of inner experiences and one's proclivity for drug use, overeating, and juvenile delinquency. In adolescents who exhibit such forms of social acting out, he noted an inability to engage in fantasy. "Their early contacts with adults never taught them to try out, playfully and in fantasy, the complex and relatively self-controlled behaviors of their elders" (p. 34).

Daydreaming is not, therefore, always an idle and useless activity students engage in solely to escape the tedium of classes. It is, in effect, an essential process in problem solving whether personal or scientific. Daydreaming is thinking that may be productive; it is conceptualizing the possibilities. For example, when I asked David, "What if all the ice in Antarctica were to melt within the next two years?" he replied:

> All coastal regions would be flooded. . .populations would shift to the middle states. . .living patterns would have to change. . .our whole economy wuld be altered. . . .

These possibilities were suggested within about twenty seconds, and then he looked me in the eye and with a sly smile added, "Venice would no longer be unique."

David's replies were not in the form of daydreams, but they reflected the same playing with ideas. His humorous comment about Venice is similar to Laura's seeing the world as an atom in the body of an almost unimaginable colossus. David and Laura do not report an extensive amount of this kind of daydreaming; they report more immediate concerns relating to the day's activities, boy-girl relations, previous experiences, or projections into the not too distant future. What is significant, I believe, is that in responding to my questions and in their dreaming during class David and Laura are engaging in a kind of thought process that takes flight from the concrete situation they find themselves in and allows ideas to "roll around in your mind" somewhat aimlessly generating possibilities and novel perspectives upon their lives and their worlds.

People combine ideas at will when they play, because they are in control of the process and can change roles and interactions with others to suit their own egos. Thus, we are intellectually flexible as the result of this cognitive restructuring of any personal, social, historic, or scientific problem we confront. And, as Singer has noted, this ability to engage in such fantasy appears to be directly related to the extent and quality of our playing as children. A David and Laura are playful physically, emotionally, socially, and intellectually because they lived rich lives as playful children.

Experimentation and Daring

Huizinga in *Homo Ludens* (1950) noted that the oldest meaning of the word play is "to take a risk, to expose oneself to danger for someone or something" (p. 39). Robert Neale's *In Praise of Play* (1969) defines play as embarking upon an adventure, "to participate in an event that takes place by chance, entails risk, and is of remarkable import." (p. 43). To be truly playful an experience must emanate from an inner peace with oneself and requires a freedom to be someone else in the everyday world, that is, to play different roles.

Trying out filmmaking with little prior experience is taking a risk, and so is adventuring into strange barns full of stranger cows! Taking a risk doesn't necessarily involve great danger; it involves pursuing a course of action with an unpredictable outcome, taking a dare, making choices to experiment. Meeting new people always involves the risk of being rejected; there is a risk in sharing a part of oneself for the fun of discovering new acquaintances.

Experimentation also involves taking control of situations and restructuring them in accordance with one's own wishes, just as David did in rifling the volley ball beneath the net creating surprise, novelty, and a new game. He took control of the rules of the game and altered them at will. Laura sits in class at times and dreams of a cross-country bicycle trip out to Colorado with her girl friends, a journey involving considerable risk and unpredictability.

Such daring and what Erikson (1974) called "leaning out over a precipice" is part of growing up and learning how to adapt to different situations, to reorient them, and to take control of them to suit one's own purposes in business or leisure.

What are the preconditions for such adventuring into the unknown? A rich repertoire of childhood dramatic play experiences allows a child to experiment in fantasy with a variety of roles and imagined problems. This further necessitates an adult-child relationship that fosters aggressiveness on the part of the child—that is, the opportunity to explore, test, and play away from too strict supervision of parents. What parents must provide is a secure, emotionally stable home base of love for a child to leave and come back to. All explorers, be they babies of two or Admiral Byrds flying over the South Pole for the first time, need a trust in the availability of help in time of trouble. Dancing down Park Avenue with your wife, to her slight chagrin or stepping out of a lunar module and onto the moon require trust in a partner's love or trust in life giving support from thousands of experts. Thus, David and Laura will continue to adventure into the social, physical, and mental unknowns so long as they feel encouraged, secure within themselves, and supported by their mentors, be they parents or teachers.

Significance for Teachers

The remainder of this book attempts to explore possibilities for tapping the imaginative resourcefulness of junior and senior high school students. David and Laura are playful individuals who use their imaginations in a wide variety of contexts and forms, not just in creative writing or the visual arts. Such imaginativeness can be developed for its own sake (while concurrently fostering abstract thinking) or used for the attainment of teachers' subject matter goals.

There are several key factors that support this assertion about the efficacy of playfulness and play for the educational process:

1. Most school experiences focus upon learning that is convergent; that is, it elicits from students correct answers, and student thinking is characterized by recalling the facts they have heard in class. What is too often overlooked is the importance of the idiosyncratic and imaginative ways of looking at problems and people, the challenge of looking for the novel solution or posing the unheard of question, of experimenting in playful fashion with roles, rules, and outcomes. There are many reasons for such emphasis upon convergent thinking—it is less demanding of teachers' time and efforts; it is easier to evaluate one correct answer than several potentially valid ones and there are many important areas in life where such thinking is required, perhaps more important than the SAT examinations.

2. A primary thesis of this book is that all subject areas within schools find their origin, not in convergent thinking, but in the imaginativeness of man. "Science," wrote Bronowski (1971) "is as much a play of the imagination as poetry is" (p. 50). This means that if teachers look beyond the search for right answers, they will find within each subject a realm where concepts are created, where thinkers toy with the impossible, where there is visual and metaphorical thinking of what is not present. These are all aspects of thinking that, according to Hannah Arendt (1977), is really imagining!

> Without the faculty of imagination, which makes present in a de-sensed form what is absent, which transforms sense-objects

into images, no thought processes and no trains of thought would be possible at all. (p. 126)

3. Research on such activities as visual thinking, creatively juxtaposing facts and ideas, and the learning process itself indicates that the imagination is *one* pathway toward creation of more meaningfulness and the improvement of achievement results for students.
4. Research, finally, indicates that student reasoning abilities can be improved by confronting problem situations. The imaginative "What if. . ." question presented in history, language arts, science and math are good frameworks for the development of logical reasoning and associational thinking.

"To my way of thinking," wrote Piaget, "knowing an object does not mean copying it—it means acting upon it" (1971, p. 15). And action may mean having the opportunity to transform information, to rearrange it, to juxtapose it with previous experiences—to toy with facts and ideas in the smithy of our imaginations. Research (Johnson, 1975) indicates that given the opportunity to create a connection between noun pairs in the form of original sentences, students are better able, subsequently, to recall these sentences than subjects who were given a linking sentence created by someone else. We all can remember our own novel productions—as a senior, Laura described in vivid detail the fantasy productions her sixth-grade teacher had orchestrated as group projects.

And we are more adept at solving original problems if we have had the opportunity to relate facts and ideas to previously learned information (Mayer, 1975). In both instances, toying with information potentially increases its significance and our ability to utilize it in novel situations in the future.

With these assertions we can now begin to look behind classroom doors to explore the possibilities of imaginative play. The play experience has been characterized as a range of behaviors from exploration of the unknown through imaginative transformation and the generation of novelty. This model is exemplified in David's exploring the unknowns of filmmaking and cow barns and Laura's imaginative flexibility within physical, social, emotional, and intellectual domains.

Most of the suggested experiences that follow focus upon how students can imaginatively transform reality thereby making it more meaningful to them.

For our purposes curriculum is conceived as the environments teachers create with students in which they explore and transform the stuff of the world—knowledge, skills, and attitudes. Curriculum is not a course of study; rather, it is a lived-in environment composed of physical structure, social interactions, teacher and student patterns of communications, human and manufactured resources, information to be learned, and means for learning it. The outcomes may be both intended by the teacher and unintended, because students act idiosyncratically upon the content and generate their own meanings.

As we proceed to examine the different subject areas it will help to visualize David and Laura as a part of these educational environments, for all activities are proposed with them in mind, as well as their peers. David and Laura may be a little better at some of these activities, but the developable skills of an imaginative and playful person are ones possessed by all students.

NOTE

1. In reading Erikson one tends to think that adolescents *do* find themselves during this "identity crisis," this process of social role play, which he perceives as the "genetic successor to child's play." Increasingly, I am of the opinion that the process of identity formation is developmentally on-going beyond one's teen-age years. Personal experience and recent studies of male development such as that of Vaillant (1977) and Levinson (1978) suggest this probability.

2

LIVING HISTORY

A HISTORIAN'S CALL to stir the imagination of youth and a teacher's perspective upon her students not as vessels or receptacles of facts but as creators of history, determiners of their own destinies, ably set the tone for this look at the possibilities of play in the study of history and social studies. In these disciplines play can dramatize or vivify particular experiences and engage the imagination, thereby stimulating an awareness of and interest in the unfolding of the human pilgrimage through the past to the present. A second function of play is to expand our rather narrow perspectives on the past by transcending our limited selves to include the viewpoints of historical personages who have been actors in the human drama.

One of my fondest memories as a teacher of New York City children was an extended dramatization of a Salem witch trial (described in detail later) where an alleged witch was perceived as guilty because a beautiful young girl charged the old woman with "voodooing" her into becoming pregnant. The girl's hysteria ("She did *this* to me," pointing to an enlarged belly) generated much

41

laughter, but upon reflection after the simulation these youngsters, themselves often the victims of unwarranted fear and prejudice, were able to empathize with the unjustly accused old woman.

By playing with time, place, action, and character students become aware that the events of history closely resemble those in their own lives. Because history is a search for understanding or meaning, and meaning is revealed through connections, relations, and associations, teachers can establish links between Salem witches or the pioneers of the Old West and today's students. History can be revealed not as a discipline about past events that must be memorized and regurgitated, but as a continuous process of establishing linkages of meaning within the past and between the past and the present. John Lukacs (Mee, 1976) considers all history a *re*thinking of the past, that is, reexamining commonly held viewpoints (i.e. that the Revolutionary War was only a fight for independence) and realizing that for every action there was an alternative course to take. Students will then perceive themselves as "history makers," decision makers with futures created from as many options as they can imagine.

Maris Hoodkiss has identified an important role for the imagination in social studies—increasing awareness of the need to take command of one's life, do and not be *done to*. The first step in this process is to step out of what Dewey called our hardened routines and outlooks by imagining how people in the past might have acted differently.

PLAYING WHAT IF

As noted earlier, play usually occurs within a pretend or "as if" imaginative framework that stimulates abstract thinking. When studying history, play involves selecting a significant incident and pretending that it occurred differently from the way history books describe. For example, if a class is studying President Wilson and the League of Nations after World War I, the teacher might ask, "What would have happened if the Senate had voted to join the League?" Students are asked to pretend that a statement contrary-to-fact is true and attempt to imagine the results.

Politicians like to avoid such "iffy" questions, but students encountering their nation's history for the first time, when asked such a hypothetical question, are required to analyze and synthesize such information as the League's composition, strengths, and weaknesses, the disposition of the American public, the nature of social, economic, and political events in Europe at the time, and so forth. In considering this "What if" question students are not *just* pretending; they are thinking about an alternative, one that could have happened. As Ms. Hoodkiss said, such questions "give the students a concept of the alternatives that life can take. . .it makes them think" in a way that asking recall questions does not. In effect, the "What if" question is perhaps an essential first step in helping students perceive themselves as participants in an historical process—as decision makers selecting among options and basing decisions upon human values, aspirations, and feelings. They can begin to conceive of themselves as history makers, and not just as history learners.

Other questions that might be considered in American history are:

What if. . .

there had been no religious persecution in England in the seventeenth century?

the colonists had not had a leader like John Adams?

Napoleon had not sold Louisiana to the United States when he did?

Lincoln hadn't been assassinated?

the Depression had occurred on the eve of Pearl Harbor?

the United States had remained basically an agrarian nation?

the Puritan work ethic had not been so powerful during our 200 year history?

no recording devices had been installed in the Nixon White House?

America had stronger economic ties with the developing black ruled nations in Africa?

There are, of course, unlimited questions teachers can ask not only students but themselves. What ought to be emphasized is that both can toy with some historical variables. As is evident in many of the questions, a negating factor has simply been added, e.g., What if Lincoln hadn't been shot in 1865? In considering the response, imagine Lincoln continuing to live after the Civil War and confronting the social, economic, and political realities that did in fact confront Andrew Johnson. One must know Lincoln's character, his interests in preserving the Union, his attitudes towards the South, and his perceptions of the Presidency. When Lincoln is inserted into the situations faced by Andrew Johnson, one immediately becomes aware of the alternatives available to each and, consequently, realizes that what *did* occur was not foreordained but was the result of men making decisions and selecting from options, just as we all do in everyday life.

There are other variables to stimulate imaginative thinking that will require students to respond to novelty and engage in problem solving of the sort requiring analysis, synthesis, and evaluation. Such variables are time, place, and character. By taking liberties with historical realities, students can look at the past in a different light and gain new perspectives upon the human drama.

What if. . .

John Kennedy had been president during the Civil War?

Thomas Jefferson had been president during the Watergate affair?

the nation's capital had originally been located in Atlanta, Georgia?

the *Lusitania* had been torpedoed during the 1960s?

Joseph Stalin had been a union boss and organizer during the 1920s?

the American Revolutionary War had occurred in 1876 when the West was being settled and the original agrarian society was rapidly becoming industrialized?

during the 1760s and 1770s the colonists had been almost entirely of one religious sect or group, relatively classless, of similar economic means, and of moderate political aspirations?

what some colonists advocated during the Revolutionary War years—limits on income, redistribution of property, equal rights for women, and abolition of slavery—had been effected legally?

The above series of "What if" questions dealing with the American Revolution can help us focus upon a few of the intricate problems one confronts when studying this very complex series of events. Historians today do not agree upon the meaning of that turbulent period and continue to offer many interpretations of what occurred and their significance:

a struggle over power and its limitations

an ideological, constitutional, political struggle and not primarily a controversy between social groups undertaken to force changes in the organization of the society or economy.

it was not democracy or principle that motivated men but self-interest, the lust for gain, with class interest. . .

the Revolution provided the first example of people getting together through delegated representatives making their own government. (Shenker, 1976)

As is evident, there is no uniform interpretation of the events that occurred during the 1760s and 1770s; therefore, it is useful for students to gain alternative perspectives upon this web of interrelated experiences. By posing thought-provoking questions, they must confront the Revolutionary era, not as cut and dried and dead, but as open to a variety of meanings. When teachers ask what would have happened had the Revolution occurred 100 years later than it did, they can focus on the fact that the West was mostly settled and could not have provided what Gary Nash called "a safety valve allowing a lot of that radical energy [calling for redistribution of political and economic power] to drain off." Without this opportunity for release of emotion, "you would have had something akin to the French Revolution" (Shenker, 1976).

By posing such problems teachers are asking students to imagine and reason just as they might do in physics with a pendulum problem (Inhelder & Piaget, 1958). It would not be difficult to use any one of these questions as a pre and post examination of students' formal thinking abilities. By posing the question of a generally classless society existing during those years, teachers can highlight the class struggle concept of the Revolution as well as the notion that colonial society was deeply divided over the issues, causing some historians to consider the War not only as a war against Britain but a civil war as well. The American experience in Vietnam during the 1960s is an instructive parallel to the Revolutionary War experience.

REVERSALS

Among the many different ways of gaining new perspectives upon events is Edward de Bono's concept of reversal, which is presented in *Lateral Thinking* (1970). "In the reversal method one takes things as they are and turns them around, inside out, upside down, back to front. Then one sees what happens" (p. 142). For example:

Columbus discovered America.

Reversal: America discovered Columbus.

From this vantage point the events of 1492 take on different meanings:

How did the current citizens of America view Columbus' arrival?

What did it mean for *their* future?

What significance did they attach to his voyages and those of his successors?

How did it feel to be "discovered?"

In view of recent evidence presented by archeologists examining human bone fossils along California's southern coast that Indians were possibly present in America long before the currently accepted date of 12,000 B.C. and that *homo sapiens* might have inhabited America before Europe, looking at the arrival (or should I say the intrusion?) of European adventurers from the viewpoint of the original denizens of the continent presents not only a fresh perspective, but a needed one as well.

Consider another example:

America's growth progressed from East to West.

Reversal: America's growth progressed from West to East.

From this new perspective students can think not only of the physical movement of pioneering settlers from East to West, but, as significantly, can consider how ideas, cultural innovations, and customs nurtured in the Far West have influenced the lives of those in other parts of the country, e.g., the discovery of gold, oil, and other minerals, the folk lore and apparel of the "Wild West," the effects of the exploitation of natural resources such as the buffalo, the showmanship of Buffalo Bill and his traveling circuses, the sub-culture of change, growth, and continuous development manifested in superhighways and freeways, fashions, and suburban sprawl, and finally, the influence of Hollywood upon the lives of children, adolescents, and adults—the romanticization of the American Dream and of young love.

Some other reversals of commonly accepted perspectives that might be considered are:

Accepted Perspective:	"We hold these truths to be self-evident: that all men are created equal."
Reversal:	We hold these truths to be self-evident: that all men are not created equal.
Accepted Perspective:	Unfettered individualism has made this country great, strong, and a refuge for seekers of freedom.
Reversal:	Unfettered individualism has made this a country where the strong dominate the weak, perpetuating inequalities found all over the world.
Accepted Perspective:	The Civil War ended in 1865.
Reversal:	The Civil War did not end in 1865 but has continued up to the present.
Accepted Perspective:	The Tennessee Valley Authority "operates through partnership with local authorities and the voluntary cooperation of individuals" (Morison, 1965, p. 963).
Reversal:	The TVA operates through government control of individual freedom with little cooperation or partnership.
Accepted Perspective:	The Federal Government controls the destiny of the American people.

Reversal: The American people control the des-
                         tiny of the Federal Government.

IMAGINATIVE QUESTIONING SEQUENCE

Educational research has indicated throughout the last two decades that most of the talk in classrooms is done by the teacher. The
predominant pattern is teacher solicitation-student response
(Dunkin & Biddle, 1974). Within such a question-answer pattern
there is room for a broad variety of kinds of questions from simple
recall to more difficult evaluative questions. It seems that many
teachers are prone to concentrate upon the recall level of Bloom's
taxonomy because they want to know if students have read or paid
attention to what they have said. Too infrequently do they challenge students to think beyond the facts, to approach a problem
from a novel perspective, or to generate a new concept.

We also know from research that asking recall questions is very
profitable in so far as student achievement of specific results is concerned. To date, asking "higher order" questions (analysis, synthesis, and evaluation) has not made much difference in terms of
student learning (Winne, 1979). This does not mean that teachers
need not ask such questions; rather it perhaps means that they
need to focus upon how such questions affect student thinking processes when they are asked (p. 45). Further study is indeed needed.

The above suggests that teachers are more comfortable with certain forms of verbal interaction. These forms are not, however, necessarily those that are best for developing the meanings students
are searching for nor for broadening historical perspectives. In an
attempt to approach these problems from a slightly different position, it seems beneficial to suggest alternatives to the traditional
question-response pattern found in classrooms. To make an easy
transition from recall of facts to a more active search for understanding of information, the following sequence, suggested by
Hunter (1972), is one I have used with student teachers and graduate students on several occasions:

Knowledge: Who discovered America?

Analysis: Why did he/they sail westward? With
                             what effects?

Evaluation: Were these voyages significant, in your
                             opinion? Why?

Imaginative: What if Columbus had landed in South
                             America or Antarctica? Suppose the
                             American Indians had sailed East in
                             huge dugout canoes?

This last question elicited this response from one of David's friends:
"We would have certain reservations about the English!"

Such a progression could not be used with every question asked,
since all do not lend themselves to this kind of probing. However,
with pivotal or leading questions that stimulate thinking about
causes, effects, and values of specific events or concepts in history,
such a progression is both logical and productive, creating an unlimited array of possibilities for thinking:

How settlement patterns develop following exploration.
The significance of the historical moment.
The views of the "hero" philosophy of history.
What constitutes an incentive or need for an exploratory ad-
venture within a particular culture?

As with all creative, hypothetical ventures of this sort teachers
start with what they think is the known—Columbus, the Vikings,
or some as yet unknown group of adventurers arriving upon our
shores—and proceed to invite students' imaginations to play with
the possibilities. One result is that they will return to the known
with fresh understandings; they will have done what Lukacs suggested in "rethinking" the past. They may see the Indians in a new
light and look upon Columbus through their eyes.

In sum, by playing with variables in the historical experience
teachers and students are not playing mildly amusing games. Rather they are focusing upon reality that, like a multi-faceted gem, is
intriguing because of the varied perspectives from which to examine
and understand it. "Historians are always focusing on some aspect

of the truth," Gordon Wood (Shenker, 1976) observed. "It's a question of perspectives, and some perspectives are limiting." This is precisely the value of play in history—to open alternative view points thereby gaining what Merleau-Ponty (1975) has identified as the "reciprocity of perspectives." Such a reciprocity ensures an intensification of meaningfulness: "To say there exists rationality is to say that perspectives blend, perceptions confirm each other, a meaning emerges" (p. 314).

Meaning emerges as we think and rethink or, as Martin Heidegger (1972) would say, as we "unthink" the past and refuse to accept what has been handed down as historical tradition or as fact without our own search for significance (p. 76).

And, finally, students of history achieve a heightened sense of responsibility for their own actions by playing these games with the past, for they become more aware of choices, of selecting from alternatives. Such consciousness makes them more aware of their own freedom to choose their own lives, their potentiality as "history makers" in control of events more often than not.

ENACTING HISTORY

When children play house, they can be observed engaging in what is called symbolic or thematic play. Pretending to be a father or mother is a form of role assumption and identification during which a child participates in a variety of mental tasks: ingesting information, sorting it out, posing problems for a partner, making decisions about problems posed by a partner, and generating responses. Smilansky's (1968) discussion of this play activity is very informative and reminds me of what actors do during an improvisation—listen to and respond to a partner in a problem solving situation. For children as well as adults, the process facilitates self-understanding and helps them cope with stressful and emotional situations in their lives. They enact situations that are very meaningful to them without fear of incurring the possible consequences of similar actions in real life. While playing they are in total or shared control of reality, and in this sense Sutton-Smith's (1975) interpretation of play as a reversal of normal control patterns is most significant.

Role playing within the social sciences can not only help drama-tize significant events, thereby vivifying them for students' memo-ries, it can also help them enter into the lives of persons who have lived, faced problems, and made decisions based upon options and limited information. On several occasions I have observed Laura enacting history. On Black Monday (commemorating the Stock Market crash) she appeared in old grey clothes, brown fedora, and a sign around her neck "Apples 5¢". During a debate on the causes of World War I she appeared in a black riding hat to simulate a German soldier's helmet, and once in ancient history she delivered an oral report on Greek medicine wrapped in a white sheet. She most definitely possesses a sense of the dramatic and can visualize herself as an actor on the historical stage. Her imagination helps her empathize with historical personages and participate in their lives.

One day in an inner-city classroom I observed a simple example of how teachers can utilize such enactive processes. Tenth-grade students were studying the Middle Ages, and the teacher wanted them to think about the Catholic Church, its message of salvation and social stability, and what it might have meant for the peasant-ry. Her approach was imaginative and provided an easy non-threatening structure for student participation.[1]

Instead of reciting from a text, the teacher invited a guest to play the role of a medieval priest who challenged students to ask ques-tions about the church, "guaranteeing" that by the end of the class they would wish to join. After this challenge, an increasingly in-tense question and answer session ensued, during which the cognitive level of questions rose from recall and information gath-ering to evaluation of issues raised. Starting with merely a few rath-er halting questions from interested students who could immediate-ly project themselves into the fantasy, the interaction pattern multi-plied as more students began to play:

What makes your church so great, anyway?
Why do people have to buy indulgences?
What about the Crusades—what do your teachings say about all the killing?
Will salvation get me a good job?

What can your church promise to make my life better right now?

The role, power, and rewards of the medieval church and its effects upon the lives of people whose status resembled that of some inner-city students were clearly dramatized even though none of them left their seats.

An additional and even more significant residual benefit from this activity was what the students revealed about themselves. Just as children will project their own feelings, wishes, and fantasies upon a role or a toy, so too might adolescents. In this case the teacher learned not only about their questioning abilities, but also about their emotional apprehensions regarding identity, destiny, and power. The situation of inner-city youth is not far removed from that of medieval farmers in terms of control over their lives, relations between the relatively powerless and the powerful, and the confrontation with the unknowns of pestilence then and economic deprivation now.

Are the real concerns of students as revealed through play important in the classroom? Yes, if you believe as I do that through play what children perceive as significant and important to them will be much more readily integrated into their structures or networks of meaning. Role playing allows individuals to play with and transfer meanings (of identity, control, destiny) from person to person in a nonthreatening yet revealing fashion.

This particular class role play session was not highly structured. The teacher asked students to imagine themselves living a thousand years ago, introduced someone who assumed the role of church authority, set the challenge, and stepped back to observe the intense interaction. Subsequent variations to this structure might have included students assuming the roles of priest, Pope, or Councils of Inquiry within a wide variety of structured conflict situations such as questioning the Crusades, inquiring about personal salvation, redressing a variety of grievances, or exploring the meaning of medieval icons in the lives of peasant farmers.

WHAT MIGHT BE

Martin Duberman, playwright and historian, once proposed in

his essay "History as Theater" (1964) that the theater be considered the setting for the drama of history. That is not so original,
if we consider Shakespearean histories. But what Duberman also
proposed was using theater to dramatize the best in human character, motives, and decisions; he wanted to dramatize "human potential," the what might be of the history of man, the best within the
human dilemma.

Some practical applications of this idea go beyond the medieval
role play session just described:

- Teachers can select with students and dramatize events that are
  significant because they do represent the human potential for
  achieving excellence in rational decision making, passionate belief, creative problem posing, or compassion toward other human beings, for example. Events can be video taped as they are
  enacted by students and then analyzed by asking: "What do you
  admire about his or her character, action, dreams of the future?
  Do you possess such qualities? What would you have to do to
  become more like _____ ?" Events in history that immediately
  come to mind include Martin Luther's affixing his 95 theses to
  the church door, Constitutional Convention debates, Woodrow
  Wilson's plea for the League of Nations, John Kennedy's han-
  dling of the Cuban Missile crisis, Lyndon Johnson's pressuring
  for civil rights legislation, and Jimmy Carter's press for energy
  conservation.
- We can combine "what might be" with "what if" thinking and
  take events such as Watergate and President Nixon's response to
  it by asking students what behavior might be more appropriate
  under these circumstances. What if FDR, Kennedy, Johnson or
  Carter had been president when the "second rate burglary" was
  discovered?

These suggestions are applicable for one question responses or
several hours' dramatization before a whole class. It occurs to me
that the theater of "what might be" could be a most interesting
reflective assignment for students, reflective in the sense that they
could be asked to think back over an administration, an era, or a
quarter century of American history or that of any country and
select those quintessential events that manifest the best of human

qualities. Students would have to search for the facts, make evaluative judgments, and become more thoroughly familiar with particular decisions made during the heat of battle, so to speak. To do this they would have to use what Laura brought to her dramatizations of Black Monday and Greek medicine—her ability to think visually and imagine the real world of another person living or dead.

One day David reflected upon the historical personages he would invite to an imaginary dinner. They included Eisenhower and MacArthur. Why? "Oh, because I disagree so strongly with the way they conducted the war. I wouldn't have done it as they did at all in many instances."

In the basement of David's home, next to his drums, is his handmade papier maché model of a battle ground complete with soldiers and tanks, a playground upon which he often relived some of the famous battles of World War II.

RELEVANT UTOPIAS

An interesting proposal related to the Duberman notion is that of the relevant utopia advanced by Lawrence Metcalf and Maurice Hunt (1974). Their curricular concern is that young people should state "their basic assumptions about society" and become engaged in planning for its improvement. They present four questions that would lead toward this kind of planning:

1. What kind of society now exists, and what are the dominant trends within it?
2. What kind of society is likely to emerge in the near future, let us say by the year 2000, if present trends continue?
3. What kind of society is preferble, given one's values?
4. If the likely and prognosticated society is different from the society that one prefers, what can the individual, alone or as a member of groups, do toward eliminating the discrepancy between prognostication and preference, between expectation and desire? (p. 141)

The authors define a "relevant utopia" as "a model of a reformed world which not only spells out in specific and precise behavioral detail contents of that new world but, in addition, provides a behavioral description of the transition to be made from the present system to the utopian one" (p. 142).

The Metcalf and Hunt model provides a workable structure within which students can confront their own values and project them into the future. There are a number of possibilities for using this model as a vehicle for establishing priorities for social planning in a local community organization or, on a broader scale, within the United States in general. Another option is to consider it as part of what is identified in chapter V as the space colony game—the establishment between the earth and moon of America's first space colony, designed to provide energy resources for life on earth. One would hope that inhabitants, as many as several thousands living in man-made environments similar to those on earth, would live in peace and harmony. However, to ensure this, the social planning suggested in the relevant utopia model should be undertaken. Cast in the future and supported by imaginative conceptions of what life might be like, the thinking involved in such a project will involve toying with possibilities and playing with ideas. Some of the social, economic, and political problems that will have to be faced in the space colonies of the future are:

> governmental structures
> rules or laws to ensure safety, individual rights, and essential human values
> most suitable patterns of personal relations, e.g. family living, procreation, marriage
> the value of human labor and rewards for production
> systems of education of the young—what will be important for them to learn and how will this be accomplished
> institutions that might have to be established to guarantee social values, and economic processes
> systems of punishments for anti-social behavior.

These and a host of other problems will have to be considered by America's next generation of pioneers as they confront the new frontiers of space, just as the settlers of the West did during

America's first century. Confronting the future in such an imaginative fashion involves all areas of human thought—social, economic, political, scientific, and aesthetic. There is no reason why youth cannot profitably engage in thinking creatively about such problems on a broad, interdisciplinary scale.

INTRODUCING ROLE PLAYING ACTIVITIES

This may all be well and good, but how does one introduce such novel experiences to students? Here are some suggestions for proceeding on a small scale:

1. Don't expect students to jump out of their seats with excitement if they have had little experience with this kind of play. They are so socialized by schools to be inactive listeners that it will require patience and modelling on the teacher's part to initiate role playing in a secure, nonthreatening fashion.
2. Start on a small scale. You might have to introduce a real life situation (e.g. parent-child or teacher-student) as a way of making students feel comfortable. You might also speak to one or two potential players before class, present an idea, and experiment with a situation prior to a large group presentation. It's best to be assured of willing participants in advance and to give them time to prepare.
3. In selecting a situation choose (or fabricate) one in which a decision must be made, a conflict resolved, or a challenge met, e.g., joining the church. Keep it simple and avoid complicated ancillary problems and subplots. The roles assumed should be few, two or three people in the beginning to avoid confusion. The conflict or situation should embody, illustrate, or manifest specific ideas, concepts, values, or skills, such as compromise, listening to another person, or sharing ideas.
4. Don't be afraid of stepping into a situation if it veers off course. If you haven't provided sufficient direction, or if the issue is emotionally charged, students are very likely to run away with it, and you ought to redirect or refocus their energies and attention.

5. Upon completion analyze what occurred. The learning value will be lost for many if they do not reflect upon what has happened. Feedback is essential for effective control and direction of an exercise. Some ways of guiding feedback sessions include:

In your opinion did the players resolve the conflict well? sufficiently? realistically?

How did each participant react or respond to new information and new situations? How did each utilize such information?

What did we learn about the conflict dramatized? about the persons who played the roles (their interests, feelings, motives, values)?

Would you have acted or reacted any differently? How? Why?

What conflicts are we faced with today that resemble the one portrayed? How are they similar? What have we seen that may help resolve such real life situations?

6. It might be interesting and instructive for students to draw up a set of evaluative criteria for such exercises, ones they can use when looking at a dramatized activity. If the exercise is video taped, students, of course, will have an accurate record of what occurred from which to draw conclusions and upon which to improve, if that is in order.

Role playing may sound like kid's stuff, or it may seem commonplace and not very interesting. You may try it once and find that students are very reluctant or that they clown around too much and want to scrap the whole process. It will be very easy to follow the latter course of action if one does not achieve intended outcomes. The same might be true of experiments with small group problem solving, for example. Teachers try it once, one or two students disrupt or are unable to cope successfully with an altered class structure, and they decide that it will never work.

This would be most unfortunate, although understandable. Role playing, like any change, will be effective only if it is introduced slowly and if people perceive a real need for it.[2] For example, all my attempts to persuade my fellow teachers to bring video tape into their classroom as an instructional medium that students would learn from and enjoy went for naught until I found one teacher who had worked with me in several filmmaking adventures and who, one day, saw how television might help her motivate some particular students. Only then did *I* perceive how much reorienting a teacher's role was involved in allowing students to take control of a video tape camera and use it creatively (refer to chapter VIII). "You know," she observed while watching her students' tapes, "sitting next to kids watching their movies instead of standing in front of them behind a desk makes me think of teaching in an entirely different way." These kinds of role changes are the most difficult to make.

SIMULATING A SALEM WITCH TRIAL

Once students have experience on a small scale with simple situations, you might wish to attempt a simulation, that is, an extended role playing situation with more complex roles, issues, informational content, and decision making. Much has been written about simulations and games by Abt (1970) and Boocock (1970), for example. Elaborate games, such as Life Career Game, Diplomacy, and Ghetto, have been developed for educational purposes. Such simulations vivify concepts and attitudes in ways that are less possible through lecture and discussion. Such dramatizations overcome the future orientation teachers tend to give to many subjects —"You'll need to know this when. . ."

By participating in games and simulations students can come to realize "that they could do more with their lives than they previously thought possible" (Boocock & Coleman, 1970, p. 352). As noted earlier and will be again in the consideration of language arts (chapter III), what is very important is that players come to realize that they *can* assume more control of their lives, that human beings need not spend their entire lives as reactors to others' demands, but that they can initiate courses of action for their own benefit and self-development.

One need not purchase elaborate games such as Life Career to engage in these activities. Any situation you select for role playing or brief dramatization can, with planning and organization, become a simulation game:[3]

1. Select a significant event, one that embodies some principle, concept, or problem whose resolution engages students in a meaningful process or set of skills. For purposes of illustration I will use a Salem witch trial, a simulation I have worked with in an American history class.

2. Define for the players the background of the problem or conflict to be resolved, the social, political, and economic factors preceding the event, and explain or determine the religious issues of Puritan Massachusetts in the seventeenth century and its values, goals, and system of rewards and punishments. In the case of a witch trial, suggest the probable or factual sequence of events preceding the simulated event.

3. Define clearly the various roles to be assumed, the special "interests" of each, what motivates the individuals, what their goals are within the situation, and any background information relating to achievements, aspirations, or feelings. In the case of a trial, the roles of the judge, state's and defendant's advocates, jury, witnesses, defendant, and observers need to be clarified, not predetermined but outlined so that within the playful context more or less realistic decisions and actions may be taken. Insure that each player has a specific objective toward which to strive.

4. Clearly define the problem to be resolved (find accused innocent or guilty of witchcraft) and the process to be used (a trial). There may also be identifiable decisions to be made prior to the reaching of a verdict (jury selection, for example) or generic decisions of which participants must be appraised, such as ruling on motions and admissability of evidence.

5. Allot adequate time for the process to be carried through.

6. Spell out clearly a set of rules for the game and procedures to be followed by participants. For example, explain how jury selection would proceed, what kinds of evidence will be ad-

missable, or what to do when witnesses refuse to testify or if there is indecision amongst jurors.

7. Consider what resources are available to each player in the form of sources of information, funds, counselors, material possessions, and the like. In the case of a witch trial, resources would include access to legal procedures practiced during the seventeenth century.

Much of the above information can be presented to participants in the form of background information sheets and personal role cards handed out sufficiently in advance to ensure adequate preparation. All the above could also become the objectives of small group inquiry; in other words, students would discuss the idea of presenting a witch trial while studying colonial history. They would determine the kinds of information required to stage such an event, divide into small task groups, do research, present findings, and then utilize this information to dramatize this aspect of our religious-social history.

The background and procedural information students might discover would be somewhat similar to the following:

Background

Salem, Massachusetts, witnessed a series of witch trials in 1692, which resulted in the deaths of over twenty people with many saving their skins by accusing others. During this era people believed that one could bargain with the devil, thereby inflicting good or evil upon others, a process rather like the witchcraft practiced by medicine men or shamans in primitive societies. People could be accused of witchcraft for engaging in any number of scandalous offenses such as premarital intercourse, adultery, blasphemy, or strange, inexplicable deeds.

Puritanism controlled the religious views of pastor and congregation alike: devotion to God and the duty to live in accordance with His laws and avoiding anything sinful such as games, which diverted one from toiling for God's glory. Man was basically sinful, in accordance with Calvin's teachings; salvation his first priority.

Religion was not a Sunday ceremony only; it permeated all

aspects of life from what one learned in school—the Gospels—to the function of government, which was to ensure the maintenance of faith in God.

The accusation of being a witch was, therefore, comparable to a high form of treason against the church and society.

Fundamental Concepts

The basic concepts that might be dramatized by a witch trial would include individual liberties vs. the public good, reason vs. passion, private citizen vs. the church's-government's control, humankind as good vs. humankind as sinful, personal self-determination vs. the church's doctrines of sin and salvation.

Roles

Roles to be played would include: the pastor, the judge, an accused witch, the accused's attorney, prosecutor, the jury, witnesses, and observers from the community.

Procedures and Rules

Procedures to be followed could follow those of a present day courtroom, since access to this process is much more readily available and part of public knowledge. Decisions to be made as the trial proceeds include jury selection, determination of witnesses, kinds of evidence admissible, kinds of questions permitted and the guilt or innocence of the defendant.

Resources

Available resources could include doctrines of church, legal procedures, historical records and novels, e.g., *The Scarlet Letter*.

Outcomes

To determine the guilt or innocence of an accused witch.

Evaluation

As is evident from the format of a simulation and the specific example of a Salem witch trial, there are many processes, concepts, and attitudes to focus upon and evaluate: the nature and influence of Puritanism, the role of the clergy, the judicial system then and now, the treatment of dissidents then and now, and conflict between individual rights and the perception of the public good. Such a trial stimulates thinking about the treatment of those who are different, a major theme in literature—*The Scarlet Letter, The Crucible* (two works related specifically to colonial America and Puritanism), *Hedda Gabler, The Merchant of Venice,* and *Black Boy,* to name only a few.

In evaluating this particular simulation the availability of video tape was most significant. First students want to view the tape of their performances, to see themselves playing the roles, interacting with each other, speaking and reacting spontaneously. Since roles are only outlined in terms of interest and values, there is much leeway for individuals to infuse their performances with the embellishments of a lively imagination. I recall one witness, a girl who affected a particularly high pitched voice, a sufficient amount of hysteria, and even a few tears as she recounted how the accused witch had done horrible deeds. The prosecutor asked her, "Now lady Jane could you give us a little bit more insight into the nature of these deeds which you are alleging?" Lady Jane stood up and screamed, "She did this to me," pointing to an enlarged belly, "She did *this* to me!" The gallery gasped in sheer disbelief as the witness was indicating an advanced stage of pregnancy. "You've all heard of the Immaculate Conception," she continued in tears, shaking miserably at her current shame. "Well, this one was *voodooed* into me unbeknownst to me or anybody else!" By this time dismay had turned to a more natural laughter from the gallery and all other participants. Needless to say, no one foresaw such imaginative play with the witch's alleged powers of influence.

As noted in discussing the priest and peasant role playing situation, an alert teacher can learn a great deal about the participants in a simulation activity; their real concerns often emerge (for example, for individual rights, belief in the supernatural), their reasoning abilities evidenced by responses to bits of evidence or legal challenges, their creative potential and ability to react imaginatively to new situations, as did the girl with the supernaturally induced pregnancy. Having a video tape that can be preserved while students proceed to other themes and other simulations could provide a good developmental picture of individual and group growth in cognitive as well as social-emotional domains. And, if possible, storing tapes in a permanent library allows teachers to utilize them again and again to excite other students to the possibilities and the fun involved in such activities. Their instructive nature is not to be overlooked either; if a game has been thoroughly researched and if participants were well prepared, a tape can provide a vivid dramatization of the personal daily conflicts engendered by such doctrines as Puritanism and such social structures as a theocracy. And how much better these individualistic, student prepared libraries of information and drama are (or can be) than those written and produced by Madison Avenue publishers!

As with a role playing situation, evaluation of the experience is essential, and teachers can ask questions about how players felt and why they acted as they did. One of the key questions ought to be "What does all this have to do with me?" Here are some responses from Jacqui and her friends:

> Sometimes I feel like a witch the way people treat me.

> There are people here in the city who believe in all that supernatural, voodoo stuff, only they call it "roots."

> Black people are still witches to some white folks.

> People often try to eliminate things, ideas they don't understand or are afraid of.

Such comments will be more meaningful, of course, if the simulation has been selected with care to dramatize fundamental-to-life concepts, skills, or attitudes. As the students noted, today's society may not burn witches, but it often responds irrationally to the unknown.

STORIES AND MYSTERIES

"I try to present history like a mystery story," remarked a friend,[4] "I am attempting to build suspense by creating within my students the anticipation, the expectation about what will happen next." The concepts of story and mystery are two effective means of enlivening history. History is the study of peoples' lives enacted on a grand stage—their stories told from the perspective of on-the-scene observers or historians reflecting upon the past and selecting information that conveys events and their meanings. The teacher who sees students as "history makers" is aware that they are enacting stories, or as Maxine Greene would say, "they are choosing themselves, their lives," and in so doing are creating history just as did Charlemagne or Henry VIII, with obvious differences in the consequences and influences of their decisions.

The story element in history is revealed when people enact collective dramas, such as the story of the Pilgrims, Navahos, American minorities, or the NASA Space team or individual dramas with plot, characterization, dialogue, and an enveloping environment. Each tells a story through the choices made. To view one's own life or that of historical personages in this fashion "is to trace a voyage, a pilgrimage, a search in a labyrinth, perhaps an endless struggle like that of Sisyphus" (Novak, 1971, p. 45).[5]

Stories and viewing history as story can become a part of the educational process in a variety of ways:

- David once told a seminar class the story of the Russian Jews and their journey from Russia to Ellis Island and to Cherry Street in New York: "Imagine yourself on Cherry Street," he said on one of the very few occasions I have heard a teacher commence a class by asking students to use their imaginations. He proceeded to help his friends visualize the turn-of-the-century environment of pushcarts, samovars, and crowded tenements.

- Embellish familiar stories with fantasy, for example, in the Middle Ages stories of popes, King Arthur, knights, maidens, and serfs abound. Enliven these imaginatively by reversing and transposing some elements: knights being rescued by a lady in waiting ("Hey you wrote this wrong!" shouted one girl in disbelief) or Knights of the Round Table visiting your school. (Another girl responded to this challenge by writing at greater length than ever before about taking a knight around her school and neighborhood in Brooklyn, showing him what she liked to do, and letting him know how he could help her vanquish some of the fiery dragons in her young life.)

• Project some stories into the future by imagining future events and consequences: how the minority populations in Africa will fare in the next quarter century, the outcome of America's search for energy independence, further explorations of space, and the evolution of Third World powers.

Carl Jung viewed his mental patients as having lost touch with the stories of their lives, the natural, intended unfolding of their choices, actions, and the meanings associated with them. What is being suggested is that through history one can imaginatively achieve a heightened consciousness of the stories of individuals and groups of people in a variety of enactive modes. In some respects, therefore, Jung's task and that of the teacher can be perceived as similar—to put people in touch with their own and/or other peoples' stories.

CONCLUSION

History, like math and the sciences, is often regarded by some as cut and dried, perhaps because of the large body of factual material most students are asked to commit to memory. Some teachers approach these subjects thinking their task is to pass along the facts to students. A teacher of college psychology recently told me she had to resort to the lecture method in an introductory class because "the students know so little right now;" this approach tends to overlook the fact that students are living psychology every minute of the day, as well as creating history.

David has told me several times that he wished for more variety in his history classes—more opportunities to question and share views with peers in order to engage in what John Lukacs calls "rethinking the past. . .for all history—indeed all thinking—consists of rethinking the past" (Mee, 1976, p. 104). David and Laura also indicated strong preference on a Renzulli Learning Styles

Inventory[6] for enacting the dramas of the past as a way of in-
ternalizing their meaningfulness. This undoubtedly has potential
for stirring the imagination of youth.

Finally, and perhaps most importantly, play in social studies
presents the possibility of students' exercising more control over
their lives. Through fantasy that is constructive they might learn
that they are indeed "history makers" and that they can change
their lives if they really wish to do so.

NOTES

1. This approach was fashioned by Marlene Nussbaum, teacher of
social studies in the New York City Public Schools

2. Refer to Richard Carlson's research (1965) where he identifies the
following variables as significant for the successful diffusion of an innovation: perceived advantage by recipients, simplicity, communicability,
divisibility, and congruence with values of recipients.

3. A simple overview of the components of simulations is found in
Dunn, R. & Dunn, K. *Practical strategies for individualizing instruction.* New
York: Parker Publishing, 1972. For more extensive coverage consult: Abt,
C. (1970), and Livingston, L. *Simulation games.* New York: Free Press,
1973. For indepth analysis of game theory consult Shubik, M. (Ed.) *Game
theory and related approaches to social behavior.* New York: John Wiley & Sons,
1964.

4. Robert Maslow, teacher of social studies, New York City Public
Schools.

5. For additional references to the concept of story consult Neale, R.
(1969), and Cox, H. (1973).

6. Renzulli, J., & Smith, L. H. *Learning styles inventory.* Storrs; Conn.
University of Connecticut, 1974.

We want to give our students the sense that they can control some aspects of their lives—Organizer of a "Fantasy Reunion"
Poetry is an imaginary garden with real toads in it.—Marianne Moore

3

FANTASY AND PLAY IN LANGUAGE ARTS

TAKING CONTROL of one's life where possible, being responsible for one's own actions, and experimenting with the "real toads" in one's life are three processes that can be fostered in the study of language arts. Students can broaden their social, emotional, and intellectual horizons by envisioning positive and alternative futures for themselves. Through such games as a "Fantasy Reunion," for example, a 14-year-old girl from Manhattan's Lower East Side saw herself ten years later as a test pilot—"When I was little, I always rode on the planes at Coney Island. I wanted to be in the pilot's seat." Perhaps she meant that figuratively as well as literally.

Language arts enrich role experimentation and a sense of control by providing the communication skills to tell one's own stories as well as to enter the lives of other people, thereby increasing self-awareness. Students read, write, speak, view, and hear about people who are enacting scenes from the human drama—whether they be Holden Caulfield or Macbeth. I have selected these two because I loved teaching them and because I have recently been stepping

67

out of my role as teacher and writer and into the lives of Holden and the Thane of Cawdor by performing monologs spoken by each.

The art of language is, at least partially, that of projecting and sharing personal and group meanings through symbols and patterns of symbols, that is, words in sentences. And play in language arts involves restructuring the elements of our communications system, i.e., grammatical rules, sentence structures, and word formations. It also involves attempts to vivify characters, themes, and conflicts in literature by immersing oneself in different roles and perceiving the world from different perspectives.

Elkind (1974) notes that adolescents seem to be "reacting to an imaginary audience," and at times I see David and Laura being conscious of an audience as they strut and fret their hour upon the stage. Laura's role playing in history is a good example.

In all these activities, teachers, if they watch closely, will observe the 14-year-old Manhattanite as well as David and Laura in their playful, secure worlds of make-believe injecting and revealing themselves as persons working out their identities, inserting themselves into social roles, and experimenting with possible futures. They will observe them revealing the "real toads" in imaginary gardens of play.

Our explorations into the possible will include word play and toying with rules about sentences and conclude with a consideration of imagery and fantasy in literature.

WORD PLAY

Learning the meanings of many words can be an arduous task for students. As children they learn words in natural conversation most of the time, but in classrooms they are often confronted with lists arbitrarily drawn up by others.

Altruizing the Egotist

Whatever the process, integrating new words into one's vocabulary can be enlivened through creative dramatics or what might be called open-ended role playing. When I was teaching in New York City a few years ago, I faced the problem of making words like egotist and altruist real to 17-year-olds who were somewhat less than enthusiastic about school. I consulted Norman Lewis' *Word Power Made Easy* (1949) for a solution. He presents words in interesting contexts by embellishing them with visual images, personifications, or stories:

> Now, let's see. Have you heard about all the money I'm making? Did I tell you about my latest amorous conquest? Let me give you *my* opinion—*I* know because I'm an expert at practically everything! This conceited boor is boastful to the point of being obnoxious. . . .He's an *egotist*. (p. 19)

> He has discovered the secret of true happiness—concerning himself with the welfare of others. Never mind his own interests, how's the next fellow getting along? He's an *altruist*. (p. 19)

Rather than attempting to memorize these two words (egotist and altruist) or simply using them in sentences, construct a simple pretend situation where an altruist encounters an egotist who is busy expounding all his many virtues. Such an encounter could follow many different plot lines; the altruist attempting to convince the egotist to see the world his way; the egotist enlisting the unsuspecting help of the altruist to boost his ego even further; the two of them establishing a personal advice and counselling service called Alter-Ego.

Students playing the roles of these two characters can in five minutes vividly portray the basic nature of each. In addition, they reveal their creative imaginations, their wit, and their ability to spontaneously interact—all developable skills if practiced over an extended period of time.

Other interesting encounters might involve:

The misanthrope and the altruist
The introvert and the extrovert
The ascetic and the egoist
The misogamist with the bigamist. (Lewis, 1949)

Recording some of these little word plays with a video tape camera will often make for hilarious viewing. But more significantly, the tapes can serve as a year's record of students' growth in vocabulary and the dramatic and imaginative skills of embellishing open-ended pretend situations with characters, plots, and resolutions of crises. Such tapes also become stimulus tapes for other groups of students ("See how much more creative you can be!") or as stimulants for a cornucopia of creative writing experiences.

As shall be noted more specifically in the next section, when students' imaginations are allowed or given the opportunity to act upon words, situations, or phenomena, teachers not only introduce novelty, but they also aid learning. Ten years after first playing with words in this fashion with students I can recall some of the situations.

"It's the visual image you must see under the words," drama teacher Stella Adler explained to her students. "React to the image. Find the idea behind the line first or you can't act. . . .Shop for that image in your imagination that makes you react with your own truth" (Drew, 1976). Learning vocabulary is not synonymous with acting; however, the principles espoused here and by Ms. Adler are the same—visualizing not only aids recall, it also helps develop one's imaginative capabilities.

Bisociation of Vocabulary

Arthur Koestler (1964) perceives the act of creation as a "bisociation of matrices" or frames of reference. Combining, for example, geological processes with personnel management problems or space travel with breakfast cereals will result in novel juxtapositions, perspectives, or solutions to problems. Creative problem solving such as that of W.J.J. Gordon, author of *Synectics* (1961), exemplifies the process Koestler describes. Other examples are found in jokes and puns: "The super ego is that part of the person soluble in alcohol" (Koestler, p. 65).

This notion of juxtaposing two seemingly unrelated ideas, of course, is the basis of the poet's metaphor ("life's but a walking shadow"). There would seem, therefore, every reason for teachers to introduce students to this process early in school so they perceive words (and word combinations) not only as labels attached to external objects or internal states or conditions, but as symbols of what is idiosyncratic in each person and of the novelty each is capable of creating.

Research suggests that if students are asked to create imaginative links between words, their retention over long periods of time will be better than if they are just asked to memorize them (Johnson, 1975, p. 430). Here bisociation can be a helpful process. For example, teachers can present two words to students—galaxy and ecstacy—and ask them to:

> tell a brief story using these words
> create a new product using the words
> imagine a person these words describe.

As in playing open-ended games with words such as egotist and altruist, students must use their imaginations to make original combinations, and in the process they create meaningful relations between words. The meaningfulness is enhanced because specific stimuli—words—are actively integrated within their networks of previous learnings (Mayer, 1975, p. 529 ff). When integrating new words into a story or description of an imaginary person, students are not engaged in rote learning but learning that requires active, imaginative play with what is already part of their general experience—definitions, concepts, skills, roles, and rules. The use of bisociation, therefore, is designed to foster more thorough understanding and a higher degree of transference to unknown and novel situations.

A game based upon Koestler's definition of creativity can be structured by using various combinations of words such as those listed below. The object of the game is to learn new words, practice the creative process and stimulate the formation of visual images as a forerunner to further imaginative thinking. The juxtapositions can be between any words—nouns and nouns, nouns and adjectives, verbs and adjectives, adverbs and adjectives, and so on.

nouns

alliteration	existentialism
atom	psychiatrist

adjectives

heterogeneous   frenetic
diversified   mellow

adverbs

unctiously   precipitously
chronically   well

verbs

philander   reify
feign   mock

The point of any combination suggested or made by students is
to seek the unusual for that will activate the search for original
combinations that are bound to be more easily recalled because
they are personal creations and assimilations with previous understandings.

Example: Combine philander, frenetic, feign, and psy-
            chiatrist into a brief story.

Solution: A young man feigned the role of a psychiatrist
            in order to capture the affections of a particu-
            lar young lady. During the session in which
            the lady was recalling her past, the imposter
            began philandering with her affections. His
            advances, uncharacteristic to say the least,
            created a frenetic scene—a patient running
            away from her doctor while recounting dreams
            of her childhood. Emotionally and physically
            spent, she hastily slunk from the premises.

As shall be noted later when discussing model building in science, the process of creating models and metaphors stimulates
thinking and reorients one's perspective about a particular object
or phenomena. So too with the bisociation of words: juxtaposing
"galaxy" and "ecstacy" or "atom" and "mellow" can create new
metaphors—"galactic ecstacy" and "the mellowed out atom."
Being able to recognize and create figurative language is essential
to verbal problem solving according to recent research[1] and may be
"the mark of genius in any field."

Gallomphing into Idiosyncracy

Just as David invented "authorophobia"—fear of the authorities —so Lewis Carroll invented the word "gallomph" perhaps from combining gallop and triumph (*Random House Dictionary of the English Language,* 1967). Sometimes the English language, as rich as it is, is rather limiting. Other cultures, for example, because of their environment or their social value system have created languages richer in variety in some respects than our own. For example, the Eskimoes have many words for ice, and the Masai have seventeen words for cattle. (Farb, 1974, p. 17). Language—words specifically —reflect a cultural point of view, and peoples have been inventive, often out of necessity (as have the Eskimoes).

Why not introduce students to the idea of word invention to increase their awareness of the vitality of language and its flexibility? Words can be viewed as human inventions that disclose both personal and social meanings. Words are not external, fixed labels for naming things, rather they can be viewed as a means of revealing one's world to another in the process of communication or dialogue.[2] Without becoming overly philosophical, I might note that if words are viewed less as static functions of or attachments to external reality and more as communicators of what is meaningful, inventing new words may become more palatable.

So, in a fashion similar to bisociating vocabulary words, students can combine the familiar (gallop + triumph) to create new words, a "gallomph," which means to move along clumsily.

Take any pairs of words, combine them, and create a meaning to fit any desired context.

verb	*verb*	*new word*
prepare	vacillate	precillate

adjective	*adjective*	
pretty	sexy	prexy
large	fat	flarge
blue	orange	blange

noun	*noun*	*new word*
ruler	vacillator	rucillator

brain	reify	brainify
tooth	wholesome	toothsome
pupil	stupid	stupil

Other blends are suggested by John Algeo in an article entitled "Portmanteaus, Telescopes, Jumbles" (1975):

beauty	utility	beautility
diplomacy	economics	diplonomics
Italian	English	Italish
slump	inflation	slumpflation
nickel	penny	ninny

Another kind of blend, what Algeo terms a "telescope," is made by "shortening the parts of an expression and condensing them into a single word, such as in, "This time of year, it gets darly. . .I mean, dark early." Other examples are:

Etymology	*Telescope*
advertising inflation	adflation
administrative trivia	administrivia
feminine seminar	feminar
flexible time	flextime
Feminine movement sympathizer	femsymp
medical evacuation	medevac (1975, p. 2)

The reader's own imagination will create many more examples of this kind of word play, and teachers can find appropriate moments to introduce students to these imaginative transformations of our language. Playing with words gives them an entree into the imaginative worlds of poets, dramatists, novelists, songwriters, and communicators in general.

Another feast of linguistic delicacies is found in Willard Espy's *An Almanac of Words at Play* (1976) in which he presents many enjoyable liberties taken with our language. Among the most humorous are Spoonerisms, or accidental transpositions of sounds:

> To a group of farmers, he began, "I have never before addressed so many tons of soil."
> One announcer asked, "Why not try Betty Crocker's poo

seep?" and another said the fog was "as thick as sea poop."
"Give me a jar of oderarm deunderant." (p. 34)

Other examples come to mind:

hi holed shes
unroaded paveway
garbacle receptages

One can imagine listening to a recorded speech full of Spoon-erisms just for the fun of it. Later, one might dissect them to decode the transpositions and discover the seemingly illogical juxtaposi-tions that often result in humor.

David enjoys engaging in a different kind of word play, one which demands rapid successive associations based upon the sounds of words. Sitting in his living room with his mother and sister, Emily, David was describing a story in which one of the characters wore a hat that was somewhat like a cossack hat.

"Cossack?" asked his Mother. "I thought that was what you call the thing we all have our feet on."

"No," replied Emily. "That's a kind of cloth bed you hang be-tween trees."

David shot back, "No that's the name of that poisonous plant." Then, in quick succession:

"No, that's Watson's partner's first name.
No, that's the Merchant of Venice.
No, that's what you call a real scoundrel.
No, that's the little thing that makes pearls.
No, that's a place like a monastery.
No, that's when you carouse around, rowdy-like.
No, that's an old car with a rumble seat.
No, that's what you cook meat in.
No, that's a male chicken.
No, that's where you go to buy shoes."

Needless to say, one needs a quick wit to keep up with such as-sociative word play.

Unfortunately (or fortunately), we cannot always be as independent as Humpty Dumpty: "When *I* use a word, it means just what I choose it to mean" (Carroll, 1960, p. 186). But we must acknowledge that his assertion that "The question which is to be master. . ." points to the idea that language is one of humankind's supreme inventions for conveying meaning and they are in control of the process. Vygotsky (1967) noted that in play a child acts as the master of language by transferring meaning from one object (train) to another (toy block) thereby controlling the establishment of meaning, as Lewis Carroll envisaged—the block becomes the train.

Of what value is word invention? If children are encouraged to be a little freer with words and to engage in the inventive process, they may minimally find it enjoyable to be masters of language rather than always being slaves to memorization. Being master would permit them, upon occasion, to feel in control of not only meanings but their language abilities. Creating words for special situations, actions, or objects (within a poem, story, or biography) may just have some transference to other processes, such as creation in writing, the arts, and even music. And finally word invention should help us retain some of our openness to the world and its mysteries, for by creating a word like "brainify" we open our eyes to a newly created reality, however small. What is being suggested is not, of course, reinventing the English language, but engaging in an inventive process, one that fosters creativity and has the potential (as does all play) of being useful in other contexts.

FOOLING WITH THE RULING

Long ago I gave up teaching grammar deductively, moving from general rule-to-be-memorized to practical application toward dealing with problems as they spontaneously arose in students' writings. However, grammatical rules are necessary and often difficult to master for certain students and presenting them as rules to be mastered may often avail. Rules are conventions used to facilitate communications between people. If we all followed Humpty Dumpty's dictum, our effective verbal interaction would be reduced to almost nil. Nevertheless, there are occasions when, if only briefly, we flaunt the rules and/or invent new ones.

Inverting the Noun

Peter Farb in *Word Play* (1974) discusses e.e. cummings' poem "anyone lived in a pretty how town" and shows how the poet turned verbs into nouns:

> he sang his didn't he danced his did.

cummings played with words and rules, not accidentally, but "as if, in order to transform the world, a transformation of the word were required" (Friedman, 1960, p. 24). So we might transform easy sentences for new effects:

> he sang his song
>> he sang his *cry*
>
> she wrote her book
>> she wrote her *birthing*
>
> they warmed themselves
>> they stayed *in the warm*

In addition to transforming verbs into nouns, one can reverse the normal order of a sentence and find new meanings:

> Sally found her cat
>> Her cat found Sally
>
> Macbeth seized the crown.
>> The crown seized Macbeth.
>
> The officer directed traffic.
>> The traffic directed the officer.
>
> The teacher taught her students.
>> The students taught their teacher.

The idea of reversal as exemplified above is extensively developed by Edward de Bono in *Lateral Thinking* (1970). In addition to sentence reversal, one can invert verbs and nouns to achieve interesting results:

> He drove home.
> He homed his drive.
> She picked the apples.
> She appled the pickings. (How do you apple something?)

John climbed toward the moon.
　John mooned his climb upward.

The seagull flew in circles above the city.
　The seagull circled his flight above the city.

The bridge spanned the river banks.
　The river banked the spanning bridge.

She whistled warmly.
　She whistled her warm.

All these examples of playing with words, transforming one form of speech into another, and inverting word orders create a different perspective upon a situation. In inverting the bridge sentence above, the focus is upon the banking action of the river, which is not the usual perspective when looking at a beautiful bridge, such as the Golden Gate in San Francisco, where the breenish* banks are equally as worthy of aesthetic appreciation.

Many more variations of the above can be experimented with. It seems logical that such fooling around with customs and rules will stimulate the poetic imagination; however, any form of writing can benefit from such inventiveness.

Fragmenting Sentences

Some teachers have spent much time correcting sentence fragments such às, "When the storm arose." or "Because it was my favorite." It is, of course, important that such fragmentations of complete thought patterns be corrected, because of the confusion that might otherwise, and often does, arise in student writings.

Instead of merely saying that such a construction is wrong or drawing a red line under it or through it, there are a number of alternatives, all of which attempt to help students deal with sentence formations in meaningful ways.

- Write poetry using only the sentence construction students have difficulty with, e.g. the fragment:

---

*brown + greenish.

> Whenever it rains,
> Because it always will you know;
> And after it all occurs whenever
> There's always time for mud puddling.

- Stimulate imaginative thinking by asking students to write sentences or paragraphs without punctuation (after Faulkner or Joyce). We often teach punctuation by giving students unpunctuated sentences, so their creating the sentences can serve this purpose as well. It may also release some of their creative energies by removing some of the seemingly unnatural impediments (rules, proper forms, and so forth).
- Imagine yourself a dangling participle (Coming round the bend, the Empire State Building suddenly appeared) and create a story about why you dangle or how to become undangled.
- Sentences often end up without verbs. For students who have difficulty using verbs, let them imagine life as any verb—to run, to stimulate, to immortalize, to fructify, to gallomph—and describe actions in the past, present, and future. Such descriptions, accompanied by a visual image, will create a longer lasting recollection of the verb and of the action involved.

Playing with words and the rules that bind them together can not be done every day. However, the ideas presented above are meant to suggest that imaginative playing with ideas, words, and patterns of interaction is often constructive when it comes to the art of languaging. e.e. cummings altered words to suit his creative purposes —to show or disclose new realities and meanings. Allowing or encouraging students to engage in more liberal (or less constrained) usage of words will not only stimulate their imaginations, but it will also create an awareness of the effectiveness of rules and the efficaciousness of bending, reversing, or negating them at times. Thus, when encountering the fragment, one response is "This is wrong. Change it!" Another is, "This is a fragment; there are a number of different things that can be done with it."

VIVIFYING LITERATURE

In my description of play for adolescents I presented Erik Erikson's notion that this period in a person's life is characterized by "free role experimentation. . .social play—the genetic successor of childhood play" (1974, p. 135). The purpose of such social experimentation is to try out various roles in the process of identity formation. Recent studies by Singer (1976) of delinquent adolescents indicated that, "Their early contacts with adults never taught them to try out, playfully and in fantasy, the complex and relatively self-controlled behaviors of their elders" (p. 34).[3] In support of Singer, who has perhaps done more research into the nature of fantasy than any contemporary, is Gardiner's belief about the possible causes of senseless crimes committed by affluent young people. Children in our society "have little opportunity for adventure, except vicariously, through watching television, something eminently unsatisfying. It merely whets. . .a normal appetite for adventure, satisfied often in former days through the dangers of exploration or the vicissitudes of a frontier life. Where is the teenage boy or girl to find adventure outside of crime?" (Raab, 1976).

Such adventure can be found not only on the prairies of the last remaining geographical frontiers—Alaska, Antarctica, outer space —but in the exploration of psychological, social, and religious frontiers that permit and encourage the free role experimentation envisioned by Erikson and the exploration of the unknown so lacking in some of the youth described by Gardiner and Singer. For schools to become a part of such social-psychological development, teachers and administrators must recognize along with my friend Joey Hinden that, "The classroom is the place where you're supposed to experiment" or where teachers encourage youth to play with possibilities and futures, an adventure that includes exploration of inner, imaginative worlds as well as external, more real life worlds.

Setting the Stage

Literature is one avenue for developing the inner world of the imagination. All writings presented to youth are not about adolescents, but they do portray persons enacting the human dilemma. In

two respects literature provides a good vehicle for play:
—as a means of vivifying the human condition
—as a structure within which to engage in social role experimentation and to play with identities.

When introducing a particular literary selection, it is enjoyable and profitable to stir students' imaginations by presenting conflict situations relevant to ones found in the novel, play, or story to be studied. For example, prior to reading *Macbeth* present students with this human situation for their consideration. An ambitious yet somewhat reluctant young man and a domineering, ruthless wife want to acquire more wealth and power within a company, organization, or community. How would they proceed? What conflicts would arise from their different personalities?

Another example is from Richard Wright's *Black Boy*. You are a parent whose child has just wantonly and without regard for life killed a small cat who was making a lot of noise in the yard. How would you show your displeasure at the lack of concern for a living being?

And for Salinger's *Catcher in the Rye* try this. You are a sensitive adolescent who has been thrown out of school for the second or third time and are alone with few close friends. What would you do?

Situations such as these are designed to acquaint students with the conflicts, problems, and individual characters found in the stories of Macbeth, Richard Wright, and Holden Caulfield. As is evident they closely reflect those in the books, yet they need not. Situations can be selected that deal with the major themes: acquisition of power, growing up alone and different in a strange culture, and the search for identity. Then again, they can deal with the environment: medieval England and the accession of royalty, the South in the 1920s and the racial problems encountered, and being alone in a large city with few close relationships or friendships.

In fact, virtually any kind of role assumption and conflict resolution activity can serve as a stimulating introduction to literature. Adolescents are often reluctant to engage in role play in front of their peers. This is natural since schools do not foster this kind of fantasy, which is an outgrowth of sociodramatic childhood play—

playing house, war, or school. Thus, we cannot always expect them readily to step into different roles and experiment with their feelings and values. One might start easily with simple verbal interaction: "What would you do if you were————?" Writing imaginative responses would be a second step in the prelude to stepping out of one's own character and into another.

In any case, reluctant adolescents will lose some of their inhibitions if they observe their teacher modelling the intended behaviors. If teachers wish students to role play, they must be willing to show them how it's done. Children learn to play by watching their peers and so do adolescents. Sometimes in teaching literature teachers focus so upon the achievement of specific results (identifying, naming, recalling information) that students end up like Ms. Adler's drama students who memorize lines, rather than creating the image and prior life experiences behind them. If literature is anything, it is an author's revelation of the human drama of conflicting values, ideas, and goals through actions of living characters. Students can be introduced to literature through activities that help them "react to the image" so they become like actors having a feeling for or a sense of who these persons are and why they act as they do. Through such imaginative play students will do more than memorize lines or read chapter by chapter as an assignment. Laura does this as she runs after school—infusing herself into Pierre as he faces battle—and as she watches her favorite "soap" on TV, she lives the characters' drama momentarily.

Here are more concrete suggestions for stimulating the imagination:

• The world's treasures of great painting abound with examples from the caves of Lascaux through Greek, Medieval, Renaissance, Baroque, and Modern art—examples of man's representation of human conflict. For example, the themes within Macbeth might be introduced using paintings by Titian (*Sisyphus*), and Goya (*The Giant*) to suggest power in human beings as well as sculpture by Rodin (*Balzac*) and Michelangelo (*David*) for the same theme. Power in nature can be exemplified by J.M.W. Turner's *Steamboat off a Harbour's Mouth* and Beethoven's *Eroica* Symphony.

- With portable video tape equipment teachers and students can create characters spontaneously—one with ambition and one with guts and few scruples—to act from their experiences within a situation that contains a clear objective—to gain power or authority, for example.
- Since mime utilizes bodily expression to convey action, motion, or feelings in situations, it can help communicate images and stimulate another person's visual thinking. A friend of mine uses mime to convey his impression of the atom and its surrounding electrons.

Once students have begun reading a particular literary selection, role assumption can be used to stimulate thought about characters and their interaction:

Once Macbeth has achieved the throne, what might he do next?

Holden confronts his sister who is concerned with his leaving school. What does she persuade him to do with his life?

Richard Wright is wrongly accused of littering the classroom floor by his teacher in front of his classmates. What would you do?

As in any imaginative assumption of roles, the benefits to the participant are an opportunity to "experience the other side. . .and to imagine the real," as Martin Buber once reflected upon the nature of dialogue (1965). If these situations are enacted without knowing how Shakespeare and Salinger imagined their outcomes, students can explore the universe of alternative actions, thus dramatizing the fact that as human beings they can choose their lives and their choices reflect different values, purposes, and feelings. In "imagining the real" feelings, beliefs, and experiences of another person, people enhance their humanity by expanding their horizons of awareness.

In structuring role play situations for both adolescents and especially adults I have found that participants reveal themselves in the process. If we gently push aside the imaginary flowers and step on a few of the make-believe weeds, we'll observe the "real toads" Marianne Moore spoke of (Fergusson, 1959, p. 8). In such fantasy situations, for example, adults have observed just how controlling they are in supervisory encounters with fellow teachers and have undertaken moderate alterations in their professional behavior.

Daydreaming

Daydreaming is the internalized form of childhood play engaged in by adolescents as well as adults.

> And as imagination bodies forth
> The forms of things unknown, the poet's pen
> Turns them to shapes, and gives to airy nothing
> A local habitation and a name.
> *A Midsummer Night's Dream,* act V,i,l.7.

These "airy nothings" Shakespeare wrote of and the "forms unknown" actually consist of real concerns people are confronting at any particular moment. Jerome Singer has called daydreaming a "basic cognitive capacity that develops naturally" (1975, p. 133), a skill akin to exploring possibilities that according to his research reach an apex in late adolescence, unless one cultivates it purposefully as I do.

Adolescent daydreams often concern matters of sexual relations or concerns about success in future occupations or roles, or they may involve seeking alternative solutions to current problems:

> A 17-year-old girl dreamt of distant solar systems inhabited by beings each of whom was a twin of a person on earth.

> A 19-year-old boy saw himself as a sheriff in the Old West upholding law and order with his band of comrades.

> An 18-year-old girl saw herself as a courtroom lawyer defending the rights of helpless defendants.

> David daydreams of victory on the soccer field by manipulating players and planning strategies; he further dreams of how to extricate himself from embarrassing situations with girls.

Such dreams help youth anticipate future roles and provide defenses for coping with frightening events (the imagined sheriff may thus be working out problems of self-confidence related to a very low reading level). They "can play a role in helping develop a sense of power and autonomy, not only over parents but in general over one's life situation" (Singer, 1975, p. 161). Because they have as yet not solidified their roles as persons or as members of society, adolescents can use daydreaming as their playground in which both to carry on some childhood pretending games and to think themselves into roles and situations they might one day encounter. It should be recalled that one of the criteria of play established in chapter I was that the individual was in total or shared control of his or her interactions within the play world, a situation different from real life. It was, further, this sense of control over one's destiny that James Coleman (1966) found missing among disadvantaged youth in his comparative study of schools. Imagining possible futures and solutions is one means of confronting this feeling of powerlessness.

How do teachers regard this form of adolescent play? They can ignore it, stifle it, or they can listen to the dreams of youth and use them as imaginative foundations upon which to build a bridge between literature and the reader, between humanity in general and each individual person.

Initial Steps

To build such a bridge between the imagination of Shakespeare, Salinger, or Dostoevsky and that of students, teachers can begin to let it be known that daydreaming is an act of the imaginative mind and as such can be valuable. They can begin by showing their own flights of fancy and asking students if they ever daydream. An easy, informal, and anonymous way of initiating the procedure in a class might be to invite everyone who wished to jot down a recent day-dream without placing a name on the paper. (Typing at home would be a better guarantee of anonymity, which is important to preserve because not everybody wishes to divulge her or his private dreams to the public.) The dreams are then collected and shared by the teacher reading from the anonymous papers.[4]

The purpose of this is to see what people dream about and to communicate the idea that such dreams are often the foundation of productive thinking, not only in the humanities but in the sciences as well. The intent is to extend and enrich one's associational and bisociational thought processes, not to probe students' personal lives.

From student dreams a list of predominant themes might be drawn up. Then the class can look at the extent and quality of the dreams with regard to length, number of characters, pretend or real, plot of action, number of sequences, number of different settings, character delineation (physical appearance, personality, and the like), and theme.

Many merely have rather fleeting dreams, sort of brief pictures floating before their mind's eye, "airy nothings" with little substance. One boy pictured himself as a general sitting at a desk signing papers with no further action and little idea of what the general was like or why he was there. By contrast, the lad who pictured himself as the benevolent sheriff in a scenario reminiscent of "The Magnificent Seven" was able to add several characters and sequences of action to his dream.

Further Steps

There are a number of possibilities for developing imaginative skills. For instance, take five minutes at the end of a class session (during which several individuals have probably let their minds go off into space) and invite students to let their minds wander. Since they have probably done this at least once already, a teacher can ask them to recapture that mental image.

Hold the picture firmly in mind. Then ask them to describe in more detail the following: physical setting, characters involved, personalities of characters, action occuring, and subsequent action as a plot develops.

Over a period of time teachers should find that students pay more attention to the content of their daydreams and that the dreams become somewhat more active and extensive. One way of checking on this is to occasionally ask students to share their daydreams with others. If teachers are supportive in establishing a positive emotional climate, dreams will be offered and perhaps even examined for their significance. After engaging in this dream building process, which is based upon how teachers improve the quality and extent of child's play, improvement over an extended period of time might be measured, by asking students to write down a recent dream and compare it with their first such exercise.

If such an activity in and of itself does not satisfy a need for producing more significant or generally accepted-by-the-public kind of results, these dreams, of course, can be stimuli for generating poems, stories, alternative life styles, and futuristic solutions to real problems.

Since teachers know that all students are not visualizers, that for some picturing events, objects, or scenarios in their minds is more difficult than for others, it will be necessary to act as a catalytic agent. Here are some suggestions to stimulate the imaginations of those who are perhaps better verbalizers than visualizers.

- Consult Richard de Mille's *Put Your Mother on the Ceiling* (1973) for examples of fantasy exercises. For example, have students visualize a favorite physical locale, describing to themselves the immediate environment in terms of sights and sounds. Then invite them to alter it and rearrange its parts.
- Think of a problem you have had recently; then imagine yourself acting out a solution and examining the results.
- From a novel sketch your perception of major themes or ideas.[5] Create graphic metaphors by combining drawn objects both real and imagined.

An excellent reference full of exercises designed to improve one's ability to think in visual terms is Robert McKim's *Experiences in Visual Thinking* (1972); more suggestions are drawn from this text and presented in chapter VII dealing with visual thinking in mathematics. For McKim "visual thinking is experienced to the fullest when seeing, imagining, and drawing merge into active interplay" (p. 7), with drawing often serving as a mirror for visual associations and images.

The possibilities for effective stimuli are, of course, limitless.

However, a consideration of the probable causes for lack of significant daydreaming might suggest other approaches. It was the poet
Friedrich Schiller who highlighted what he saw as two
dichotomous functions within the human mind—the sensuous and
the rational—what Nietzsche later identified as the Dionysian and
Apollonian. Too often, noted Schiller, the rational aspects of man
controlled his mental life; therefore, he advocated that occasionally
such constraints be removed from thought processes so that original, freely associated ideas could be spawned. It may have been
Schiller who first called attention to what is called "associative
play" with ideas, or in its more commercialized form brainstorming, creating within the brain a flurry of ideas and solutions to
problems without the restrictive voice of reason saying, "That's im-
practical, impossible, too costly. . . ."

Thus, for those who are not fantasizers by practice exercises in
brainstorming might improve fantasy life. Research indicates that
brainstorming is an effective technique to generate ideas, and its
efficacy in small group problem solving processes is well
documented (e.g., Miles, 1959):

- Identify a real, manageable problem within the school, community, or nation and brainstorm solutions. Stress quantity, not
  quality, of solutions to stimulate imaginative thinking.
- Take any short story and before the climax or ending has been
  revealed, generate as many imagined solutions as possible.
- Take a real object—pen, used tire, desk, television set, whatever
  —and generate as many alternative uses as possible. Stress unheard of applications.[6]
- Imagine yourself a resident of a space colony and imagine all
  possible shapes for the colony's exterior, possible land environments within its transparent walls, possible patterns of human
  relations and interactions, and the like.

Combining brainstorming with an occasional exercise in drawing
some of the suggestion solutions (as in the alternative uses for a pen
example) will reinforce the relationships between seeing, imagining, and drawing.

Any of the above suggestions should not be attempted without conscious purpose, that is, their value is substantively lost on the young dreamers if these activities are not part of an on-going attempt to upgrade the value placed upon the powers of imagination, specifically upon daydreaming. To engage in these activities once or twice without follow up, without leading to more advanced forms of explorating daydreams and their extent and possible meanings, is to waste time and is only a half-hearted attempt to recognize a significant cognitive process.

As Schiller would have stated, once ideas are generated, people have an equal obligation to evaluate their worth. Students should be afforded opportunities for engaging in the second phase of problem solving by holding each idea up for scrutiny and determining which are best, feasible, interesting, or worthy of recognition and possible implementation.

Picturing Macbeth

Recently an English teacher told me, "The problem is that so many students can't picture any of these people or places they're reading about." Struggling with alien persons and territories becomes burdensome and boring. Students have not found ways of entering the lives of Holden or Macbeth and developing a sense of identification with the problems they face.

Current investigations on the value of visual thinking for learning seem to indicate that utilizing mental imagery can significantly affect the ways students think about literary characters.[7] Young students (Einstein, for example) who have difficulty learning solely through listening and speaking can enhance their memories and productive thinking abilities by conjuring up and developing images (see chapter IV). With time and practice these capacities to create and elaborate upon images can be improved and, for some of us, so will our abilities to solve problems such as "What might Holden do if he met the movie actors he talks about?" Dealing with such a problem on an entirely visual level calls into play our perceptions of Holden up to that point and, together with our reasoning about his character, leads us to more comprehensive

projections. Thinking logically as well as spatially and aesthetically
should go hand in hand, just as they do naturally in our minds (see
chapter V).

How do we tap such reservoirs of visual thinking when dealing
with the mysteries of Dunsinane Hill?

- Before reading *Macbeth,* invite students to picture in their minds
  a castle, its surroundings, and inhabitants. What does it look like
  outside, inside? How are people dressed? What do they do during the day? How do they eat? work? play? defend themselves?
- Entertain hypothetical situations such as how rulers would respond to a group of dissatisfied peasants or how princes might
  conspire to acquire power.
- As the characters of Macbeth and Lady Macbeth emerge, encourage students to picture them in their minds, physically
  within specific settings, and share what they see. After Macbeth
  receives the prophecies, have students fantasize responses of
  Lady Macbeth: what would she say? how would she look, feel,
  act?
- Use fantasy for its natural function as problem solving: how
  could Birnam Wood come to Dunsinane Hill? With resistance
  mounting, how would you maintain power?
- Use role playing and television to capture some of the students'
  imaginings and projections.

By means similar to these teachers can enable students to picture
what is occurring without showing them the Maurice Evans film.
When there was only radio to listen to, each of the voices, the Lone
Ranger, Green Hornet or The Shadow, had a visual counterpart of
one's own creation that was conjured up every time the program
was heard. Now with television we watch Hollywood's or Madison
Avenue's visual creation. And even though Laura would claim that
there has been no effect on her imagination, I would bet her internal picture-making capacity is somewhat under utilized and under developed because of the amount of television she and everybody else watches.

Macbeth in Congress

In the previous chapter I spoke of reversals (America discovered Columbus) and playing with givens as a way of generating alternative perspectives upon historical events and stimulating formal thought. Of course we can imaginatively play with any of the givens of situations in literature as well, the givens being time, place, character, personality, action, and motivation:

- If Macbeth were a member of Congress, how would he become President?
- What would Richard Nixon do were he the recipient of the three witches' prophecies?
- Translate the witches brew into "street talk."
- How would Holden Caulfied cope with the sexual freedom of the 1970s or the political activism of the 1960s?
- Suppose Raskolnikov were an inner-city school dropout who had a grudge against the principal.
- Provide alternative endings to any play or short story plot.
- Suppose Richard Wright had grown up, not in the South of the 1920s, but in Tsarist Russia or in feudal Europe as a peasant.
- Imagine Serpico as a member of Nixon's White House staff after Watergate.
- Suppose Antigone had been accused of being a Salem witch.
- Imagine an encounter between Stephan Dedalus and e.e. cummings, Paul Cezanne, or B. F. Skinner.

As noted previously such fanciful toying with the givens of a situation is the very nature of play—children's or adults. It is worthwhile to cultivate the imagination—the poet's and novelist's "realms of gold"—and to explore the world of the possible, characters and their actions, and perspectives different from traditional ones. With the onset of abstract, or formal, thinking adolescents become much better at examining characters and their actions from a multitude of angles; there are, for example, many reasons why Holden might be concerned about the ducks in Central Park during winter. Playing "What if" and recombining some of the variables mentioned provide a framework for enhancing students' transition from concrete to more complex reasoning.

Resynthesizing Childhood Memories

Many adolescents (and adults) do not use their inner resources to explore, playfully and in fantasy, the new roles of oncoming (or continuing) adulthood. With the pioneering work of Daniel Levinson (1978), which revealed the different "seasons of a man's life," it seems logical to me that throughout life there ought to be opportunities for all of us to learn how to imagine new social roles, to playfully question social rules and institutions, and to experiment with alternative futures. In those transitional periods of our lives, such as adolescence and the so-called "mid-life crisis," it seems appropriate to structure for students (and teachers) occasions for imaginatively "leaning out over the precipice" of new roles, and this can be done within classrooms.

For example, I once gave students the opportunity to work on problems they faced in a life skills class based on the work of Winthrop Adkins of Teachers College, Columbia University. The content was student controlled, and in both instances real sources of conflict were identified: establishing independence from parents and establishing responsible relations with employers who seemed to take advantage of them. In these situations the following procedure was developed along lines suggested by the Adkins model:

- A situation was outlined, e.g., student returning home late to angry parents.
- Select four-five students to respond to the situation and offer their own solutions, e.g., upon returning home, how would you react to your parents? Role play the situation before a video tape camera and ask players in this scenario to wait in the hall while the others enact their solutions. This way two or three different solutions can be recorded.
- Play back solutions for analysis and critique. Have students develop their own criteria for successful resolution of this conflict and compare alternative solutions presented by different players.

Once with this particular problem, one girl who played the role of the mother stepped into her part a little too effectively and unleashed such a torrent of abuse upon the unsuspecting teenager that I had to stop the dramatization. She had, evidently, recalled bitter memories about her own situation and became almost uncontrollable in her rage (to the sympathetic delight of her friends); on this occasion I shied away from scrutinizing these too real toads.

Fantasy, like play, is no respecter of class or economic status, and there are teenagers from less than privileged neighborhoods who have experimented with imagining alternative futures to regain a sense of control over their own destiny. Through fantasy, girls ages 10-17 in a program called Discovery and Awareness for Women Now, have begun to realize that poverty and passivity are not always necessary elements in life; they need not be victimized by them for the rest of their lives. One of the girls' leaders in this program commented about an activity called the "fantasy reunion" in which girls imagined returning after a decade in their desired roles:

> Most girls in this neighborhood grew up feeling that whatever happens to them happens without control. Kids here become pregnant out of passivity; they drop out of school out of passivity. . . .We want to give them the sense that they can control some aspects of their lives. . . .My definition of feminism is to be an "actor upon" rather than the one acted upon. (Brozan, 1977)

When these girls play, they become aware that they can do more with their lives and need not accept victimization from those with more power and economic security. As Maris Hoodkiss observed about fantasy and history, students learn that there are options from which they can choose. The girl who as a child played on the planes at Coney Island and at age four wanted to be a test pilot may or may not realize her dream, but without the dream she might languish in the tragic cycle of passivity. Restructuring one's life in accordance with one's own wishes is part of the risky adventure of play.

CONCLUSION

Language arts learning can be a form of expressing one's own meanings in dialogue with others, and at times these meanings may be as original as those created by David, Lewis Carroll, or e.e. cummings. It can be more than memorizing lines and outlines of plots if teachers heed the advice to seek the image behind the lines and to find those experiences in students' lives that enhance their understanding. Here is where Laura's emotional imagination might be most advantageous by helping her establish a connection between her own hopes, feelings, and goals and the lives of the people she reads about.

But these processes are not the sole province of the arts, for as Bronowski (1971) noted, "Science is as much a play of the imagination as poetry is."

NOTES

1. Pollio, H. R., & Smith, M. K. *Metaphoric competence and complex human problem solving.* Unpublished manuscript, University of Tennessee, 1979.

2. The notion of language as more than labeling and naming of referent objects is drawn from Heidegger's *What is Called Thinking?* New York: Harper & Row, 1968, and Dwayne Huebner's exposition of this and other Heideggerian works in his essay "Language and Teaching," unpublished manuscript, Teachers College, Columbia University, 1968. Language is not merely an instrument; "language sustains man, opens up possibilities for being-in-the-world, comforts him, preserves truth, and provides the platform to jump momentarily beyond himself" (Huebner). See also Pinar, W. (Ed.) *Curriculum theorizing: The reconceptualists.* Berkeley: McCutchan, 1975.

3. Singer finds evidence of such a lack of inner resources not only in delinquent adolescents but in adults as well. He also found such a paucity of imaginative capabilities in overeaters, who "experienced significantly less visual imagery in their fantasies," and in drinkers and users of hard drugs whom Singer characterizes as "people who have failed to develop an elaborate and satisfying inner life. . .Lacking the ability to try out, in fantasy and with impunity, a range of possibilities, they seem to be the victims of external forces. . .They lack the inner control and quiet sense of purpose that a rich imagination can provide."

4. A somewhat less formal way is suggested by Frank Cocuzza, English teacher from West New York, New Jersey. In discussing Macbeth's imaginings ("that suggestion whose horrid image doth unfix my hair. . ." I, iii l. 148) about acceding to the throne, he inquires about the nature of such a mental activity, daydreaming, and proceeds to ask how unusual it is for persons to behave in this manner. Using a fictional character as a stimulus for the discussion of daydreams may initially be less threatening.

5. This idea was suggested by Sara McGinty, Chairperson, Department of English, Millburn High School, Millburn, New Jersey—she engaged her students in creating a giant mural of the salient themes perceived in *Moby Dick*.

6. See Torrance, E. P., (1966).

7. Patten, B. *Mental images and modification of learning defects*. Paper presented at the annual meeting of the Orton Society, Dallas, Texas, November 9-12, 1977. (ERIC Document Reproduction Service No. ED 151 746). See also Salomon, G. Internalization of filmic schematic operations in interaction with learners' aptitudes. *Journal of Educational Psychology*, 1974, *66*, 499-511. A very important discussion of the developmental characteristics of visual imagery is found in Fleming, M.L. *Sensory vs. symbolic aspects of imagery processes*. Paper presented at the annual meeting of the American Educational Research Association. New York, April, 1977. (ERIC Document Reproduction Service No. ED 142 970). Fleming asserts that verbal and visual processes are two different types of cognitive representation which develop concurrently along very similar lines reflecting a child's development from a concrete thinker to one who can think hypothetically, who can actively manipulate and transform images as he does variables in a physics experiment. Such imagery production can enhance learning of concepts for children and adolescents; much more research is needed.

The words or the language, as they are written or spoken, do not seem to play any role in my mechanism of thought. The psychical entities which seem to serve as elements in thought are certain signs and more or less clear images which can be "voluntarily" reproduced and combined. . .this combinatory play seems to be the essential feature in productive thought.
—Albert Einstein (1955)

. . .science and literature, science and art, belong together as matched halves of what is unique in human experience.   —Jacob Bronowski (1971)

4 ───

COMBINATORY PLAY
IN SCIENCE

THE RELATIONSHIP of science, literature, and art can immediately be illustrated by the thinking processes of Albert Einstein. For the man who formulated special relativity in 1905 and general relativity in 1914 the most important kind of thinking was exemplified by his famous thought experiments, or *gedanken*. At age sixteen he was concerned with the problem of explaining the nature of light in accordance with Newtonian mechanics. He therefore imagined what he would see were he to ride along a ray of light and observe the properties of that beam. Would he see a wave in motion or motionless crests as if one were riding atop an ocean wave? (Whitrow, 1967, p. 11). How could a beam of light observed from space "appear as a spatially oscillating electromagnetic field at rest?" These concerns led him to study the motions of the speed of light with respect to the relative motion of an observer and the measurement of time, specifically, the occurrence of simultaneity. Einstein's challenge to classical concepts of space and time was, therefore, fostered not by dogged pursuit of experimental results, but by allowing his imagination to consider impossible conditions in order to arrive at better understandings of natural phenomena.

Neither David nor Laura is an Einstein, but their minds work in similar fashions. For example, I once asked them, "What would happen if the sun split in half?"

"You mean it just split in two and stayed within the solar system," David asked, "it didn't self-propel itself out into the Milky Way?"

"Yes."

"Well," he said grabbing my paper and pencil and commencing to sketch out the possibilities. "If the earth continued to revolve between the two suns and weren't thrown off into space, you might see this happening, I guess." He proceeded very quickly to describe how portions of the earth would receive so much light compared with other sections.

"The earth couldn't go around both. . . .If it went around one, only one half of earth would get darkness at any time. Here [between the suns] there's no night time. When it rotates here [180° away] you get one half night time. . .so possibly it depends upon the rotation and that would screw up half the world. . . .It'd be weird. . . .Also the sudden split of the sun might just rip earth in half."

When I asked Laura this question, she spun off another possibility—that one half of the sun self-propelled itself off into the universe thus leaving the earth much colder. When she conjured up David's solution of the earth surrounded by two suns, she began a set of logical deductions that focused upon an entirely different aspect of the problem:

"In Norway people might become less afraid of the dark. . . .you'd never have to worry about blackouts. . ."

David and Laura were quick to visualize the effects of a splitting sun, a problem others have speculated upon as well.[1] They easily generated several possibilities and drew logical conclusions from each. This required them to analyze the problem, infer consequences, predict future occurrences, and evaluate results. Asking such questions provides students with opportunities for thinking abstractly (Inhelder, 1958) through combinatory play with ideas. Of equal interest perhaps, is what such a question reveals about the interests of the students: Laura's association with the people of Norway and their feelings about the dark reveal a sensitivity to the human condition not present in David's more abstract answer. Once again, we have discovered some of the "real toads" within the imaginary garden of a hypothetical science question.

Visual thinking in clear images can contribute to our understanding; it is a way of imagining what we cannot see. We create such pictures and models, for example, when we refer to black holes, quarks with color, charm and flavor, the old solar system model of the atom, and electrical current that flows through wires and sets up a magnetic field. Creating images in the form of pictures or physical models is an act of the imagination akin to the creation of $E = mc^2$ (a mathematical model), Keats' "Beauty is Truth, Truth Beauty" and Michelangelo's *David*.

> The invention of these ideas and their interplay in language is imagination—the making of images inside our heads. In this sense science is as much a play of imagination as poetry is. . . .So science and literature are different, but they are vastly more alike than they are different. For what makes them different is their expression in action, but what makes them alike is their origin in the imagination. (Bronowski, 1971, pp. 58, 82)

Thus the imaginings of David and Laura are the foundations upon which are constructed the various school subjects they study; more significantly, their playing with ideas represents the process through which all human culture has been invented, a theme fully delineated in Huizinga's *Homo Ludens* (1950).

In this chapter I will look at science teaching from the perspective of imaginative thinking. The point is not to find better ways to remember myriads of facts, although I think it could certainly serve this purpose. Rather, my intent is to disclose possibilities for expanding awareness of and wonder about the natural world, to gain fresh perspectives upon the facts at hand, and perhaps to generate original speculations. All play is potentially mean-ingful for children and adults, and in science combinatory play with ideas results in new associations such as Laura's thinking about the Norwegians. These associations help establish new meanings, for they create a network of linkages or connections much like a telephone switch board.[2]

The activities suggested in this chapter—generating original per-spectives through playing with ideas, developing visual models, and the space colony game—represent the kind of science lived by astronomer Carl Sagan:

> Someone has to propose ideas at the boundaries of the plausible, in order to so annoy the experimentalists or observationalists that they'll be motivated to disprove the idea. . . . There would have been no search for large forms of life on Mars, . . .if I hadn't pushed for them. (Cooper, 1976, p. 49)

Proposing ideas at the boundaries of the plausible may not help students pass their college boards in chemistry or physics, but it might achieve what Bragg perceives as the essence of science, "not in discovering facts but in discovering new ways of thinking about them."[3] New ways of thinking ensue when we imagine ourselves riding along a ray of light or sitting on the sun to speculate upon the geocentric or heliocentric nature of our solar system. Science, there-fore, requires as much *re*thinking to gain new perspectives as does history. Science education should not be the dissemination of in-formation as much as fostering within students curiosity about the natural world that results from imaginatively playing with ideas and possibilities. Information may be obsolete by graduation time; the imagination necessary to rethink the information will not be.

COMBINATORY PLAY WITH IDEAS

As Einstein's decade of intellectual struggle with his thought ex-periment attests, posing problems does not always produce satis-factory answers. Robert Geroch, another physicist, observed how science isn't composed of neatly packaged answers to questions:

A common misconception among students is that physics is sharp, clear-cut, and dried. It probably comes from the way students are trained. One has to do problem 17, and problem 17 has an answer. Maybe that's what's wrong with the way we train people generally: problem 17 has an answer. Physics isn't like that, and life isn't like that.

Students ask questions as if you're going to answer them. And in science you don't normally answer questions—you try to say how one normally thinks about such matters.(1976, p. 23)

Yet in schools teachers very often ask questions to which they know the answers. Should a student ask, "Why are there so many subatomic particles?" or "What if the earth stopped rotating?" many teachers might think such questions frivolous and not give them the recognition they deserve. By asking such seemingly impossible questions the student is mentally playing with possibilities as was young Einstein. A high school science teacher once told me that he regards such questions as nuisances, as attempts by students "to waste time, to gain attention, or get the lesson side tracked onto a digression." He also considered such questions, which, he admitted, arise often in his physics classes, as "an example of this kid's inability to accept reality." Such questions can be bothersome when teachers are looking for specific answers or when they have so much material to "cover."

However, if they look a little deeper at such seemingly unanswerable queries, they will see that the students posing them are actually thinking very creatively about a problem. Perhaps playfully suggested, a question about the earth's rotation reflects a willingness to extend the limits of conventional concrete understanding —the kind of stepping out of the accepted frames of reference required for Copernicus to move beyond Ptolemy, Einstein beyond Newton, and perhaps Sagan and his colleagues, who entertain the possibility of exobiology, beyond their more conservative, earthbound contemporaries.

Such questions may inject us into the unknown—"What if the Antarctic glaciers all melted?"—into the seemingly impossible— "What if the sun burned out?" or "What if the human body did not contain so much water?"—into the purely speculative—"What would happen if the world's protective layer of ozone were one half as extensive?" and into the seemingly ridiculous—"Suppose the earth spun in the opposite direction?"

More practically, "what if" questions provide a stimulus for developing more complex-than-recall thinking. Just to cite one example: What if the earth stopped rotating? The results of such an improbable phenomenon require analysis of the effects of the earth's daily rotation on its axis, day and night, lengths of time, climate and weather patterns, magnetic fields, and much more.

Next conclusions must be drawn based upon these effects. If the seasons did not change in various parts of the country, then certain additional effects would be felt. If one portion of the earth faced the sun for extended periods of time, then other effects would be observable. If time reckoning procedures were upset, then age old patterns of calculation would have to be replaced.

Answering such questions will help students gain new and different perspectives on their world and on such phenomena as the effects of gravity upon the moon's revolution about the earth and the measurement of time and weight upon earth. Entertaining such a ridiculous question involves them in the very nature of formal thought and the scientific process. They formulate hypotheses, which Piaget and others say most adolescents should be able to do. Teachers know that some cannot and that many curricular options in schools do not encourage opportunities to engage in this kind of thinking. Such seemingly inane questions will stimulate hypothetical thinking just as it does for scientists such as Sagan.

The inferences and variety of possibilities logically deduced are infinite; here are more examples. What would it be like to have more than one sun in the sky? Instead of considering the sun-splitting question from the celestial point of view, as David and Laura did, put the students on earth. They might answer, "Shadows would become a little confusing. . .sundials would be even more obsolete. . .growing seasons would be longer. . .the energy shortage would be lessened. . .myths and cults would develop about the existence of two suns. . . ." The last conjecture Asimov (1972, p. 106) posed as a possibility for the origin of the Promethean myth of the god who stole fire from Zeus; perhaps the ancient Greeks observed two suns similar in brightness to Alpha and Beta Centauri, a present day double star.

What if the amount of nitrogen or oxygen in the atmosphere, or the temperature on earth were altered? How might life as we know it on earth vary? How might life have evolved differently on another planet with differing amounts of the critical elements?

Altering elements within our biosphere allows students to speculate about how biological organisms that have adapted to such environments would be different. Such thinking is engaged in as part of our search for life on other planets within our solar system (Sagan, 1973, p. 41 ff).

Then, too, students can make logical responses to questions without predictable answers. They may be the kinds of questions Geroch would at times prefer to question 17. The possibilities are limited only by teachers' openness to imaginative thinking and playing with variables in the playgrounds of their minds. Some questions that force students to open themselves to different ways of looking at the world are:

> What if. . .
> subatomic particles could be controlled by thought waves?
> you could control the angle of the earth's rotation?[4]
> you could increase pressure without doing work?
> water were absorbed through leaves, instead of through roots?
> blood were pumped by the heart at one half the present rate?
> organic and inorganic matter could be combined?
> you could exceed the speed of light?
> you could harness the force of gravity?
> lava were cold?
> your stomach were located in your arm?
> seaweed could produce energy?
> the natural tendency of entropy were to decrease, not increase?[5]
> the physical forces and laws operable in dropping a plate

onto the floor and smashing were reversible?
there were no water cycle?

These questions help students challenge traditional thinking, which is what they must do to progress and grow. I once asked Laura, "What if we discovered living creatures within the atom?" Her reply came quickly, "Oh, we'd have to change our language— couldn't use the word IT to refer to inanimate objects. . . .Religious cults devoted to these beings might spring up." These questions turned process into content as Laura demonstrated when she continued, "It makes me ask what if our solar system were just an atom in the body of some gigantic creature?" From one hypothesis she generated another, "It's like the old box within a box game, you know?" Suddenly the question assumed more meaning for Laura as she related it to one of her childhood toys, and revealed her ability to think abstractly.

After discussing these possibilities with the science teacher mentioned earlier—the one who was impatient with "what if" questions—he concluded that, "There's the possibility of structuring teaching toward the "what if". . . .It seems to me the natural environment presents a very good opportunity for this." In fact, he had been playing with the possible and implausible all along but had not recognized it as such.

Playing with the impossible in this manner involves thinking from very simple recall of information to much more complex analyzing, inferring, hypothesizing, and evaluating. Science education can involve all these if teachers permit themselves to propose the implausible as well as to present the well known.[6]

IMAGINATIVE QUESTIONING SEQUENCE

There are times in my supervisory and curriculum development work with teachers when I suggest preparing for a class a set of questions that involves a range of thinking from remembered facts to imaginatively playing with them. For example:

Knowledge: What is the water cycle and how does it work?

Application:	Were you building a space colony, how would you take it into account in designing the land configurations?
Analysis:	What are the effects of this cycle upon weather, topography, plant life, and the like? Why does it rain?
Imagination:	What if the cycle proceeded at one half its present rate? Suppose water *only* evaporated. What if radioactivity affected the cycle? What if we could alter its rate of progress?

This example brings into focus the importance of the water evaporation and precipitation cycle for ecological balance. Furthermore, it stimulates productive thinking about the effects upon weather and ecology of man-created pollutants such as the by-products of combustion and radioactive fallout.

This sequence, based upon Bloom's taxonomy (1956), is adaptable to any subject at any level and when thought out in advance, it can create a tightly controlled exploration of students' understanding of facts, ideas, and concepts. (See chapter II for further development of this idea.)

PLAYING WITH METAPHORS AND MODELS

"Do you have a picture in your mind of the atom, Laura?"

"Oh, yeah, sure," she replied.

"Picture yourself in or on this atom—what do you see and hear and feel?" Using de Mille's *Put Your Mother on the Ceiling* (1973) as a framework, I guided Laura's fantasy.

"O.K. I see myself on this very solid nucleus. . .with an electron out there zooming around it. . .taking many different paths. . .protecting it. . .going very, very fast. . .I heard whirring, vibrating sounds. . ."

Laura was reporting her model of the hydrogen atom fashioned after the thinking of Rutherford, Bohr, and the quantum physicists. She saw the atom *as if* it were similar to the sun and its planets whipping about in orbits with only a probability of being at a particular point in space at a certain time. Laura's imagining such a model is like Shakespeare's characterization of life as a "tale told by an idiot" (*Macbeth*). In both the model and the metaphor there is not only a certain degree of unpredictability to life at the micro- and macrocosmic levels, there is also the creation of a visual image to help us understand what might be difficult to comprehend.

What is a model? Barbour (1974) defines it as a "mental construct" or representation of reality "invented to account for observed phenomena" (p. 38). Perceiving the atom as being like planets orbiting a sun is a physical model, albeit a very old one now. Characterizing the interaction of gas molecules as being tiny elastic spheres colliding like billiard balls is a theoretical model. A wind tunnel is an experimental model, and $E = mc^2$ is a mathematical model. This process of model building has been defined by science educators as "devising a mechanism, scheme, or structure which will act or perform as if it were a specific real object or event" (Center for Unified Science Education, 1974).

Without models we would have a difficult time picturing electricity, which flows like a current through a wire creating a magnetic field composed of waves radiating from the wire. I am always fascinated by the fact that the originator of the field concept, Michael Faraday, was quite poor at arithmetic but exceptionally gifted in visual thinking.[7]

Models often suggest a theory such as the kinetic theory of gases, theories that not only interpret reality but, like general relativity, can direct attention to the bending of light from stars about the sun during an eclipse. As Einstein once remarked to Heisenberg, "It is the theory which decides what we can observe" (1971, p. 77). Models can also help solve real problems by simulating physical processes, such as wave and tide movements in a scale model of a harbor for designing flood control and drainage systems.

It appears to me that models give teachers an excellent entree to students' imaginations, not only through Faraday's or Maxwell's ideas, but by challenging them to create their own. Assuming that being able to picture unobservable or rather abstruse phenomena is a significant process, at various times teachers might encourage students to create models. For example, in the Science Curriculum Improvement Study (SCIS) materials there is an opportunity for sixth graders to explain the operation of simple mechanical systems such as a vending machine. Imagine the internal mechanism that causes candy to drop out when a coin is inserted.

Here is how such a process of model building might operate.

1. Identify a physical phenomena or process, for example, the ecological systems that interact and interrelate dependently within a biosphere—the plants, animals, river systems, earth configurations, and air masses of the Everglades.
2. What are some of the key concepts within this system?
   interdependency   cohabitation
   balance   life cycle of birth, life, and death
   mutual support   internal control
3. What might this system resemble?
   an interlocking jig saw puzzle?   a spider's web?
   the operation of a steam engine? any cybernetic system,
   a good marriage?   such as a thermostat?
                                     running a farm?
4. Which model fits the facts best?

Clearly, the interdependencies, balance and, internal control of a system like the Everglades are more akin to a puzzle, a cybernetic system, or a spider's web. The element of exterior, human control in a steam engine and in running a farm differ significantly from the internal control and self-regulatory possesses found in a system like the Everglades before it was affected by human interference. A good marriage possesses the important characteristics, but like so many ecological systems today, it is forced to react to many external pressures. Perhaps more aesthetically pleasing is the image of the spider's web. "In a spider's web each strand pulls on other strands, but the other strands also pull back. There is a balance of pulls that keeps the web firmly stretched. In the web of life also, each organism seems to be in some kind of balance with other organisms" (Haynes, 1973, p. 25). If teachers accept this as a working model, they could then use it to see where in our ecological system there exists this "balance of pulls" or balance of life forces found in a web. Once created, models should help students perceive in different ways and look for unthought of relationships.

This four step process (1. identification of phenomena, 2. description of basic elements [ideas and concepts], 3. search for resemblances, and 4. evaluation of the fit) might be applicable to almost any physical process or natural object such as:

Identification	*Basic Elements*	*Search for Resemblances*
decomposition of uranium	energy release disintegration transformation to new element	burning of wood soil erosion dandelion seed disbursement caterpillar metamorphosis
photosynthesis in leaves	absorption of energy transformation of light energy to chemical energy	electric transformer engine converting natural fuels to energy solar energy cell
earth's crust	slow drift layering flexibility eruptive	Arctic ice floe crunching cloud layering cake layering scales on a fish

In attempting to find a model for the radioactive decay of any element such as uranium, I have focused upon the basic concepts of energy release through loss of electrons and the disintegration or transmutation of one element, for example U^{235} into Thorium^{231} through the loss of one alpha particle, the nucleus of a helium atom. Looking at the resemblances burning wood was selected because it gives off energy in the form of heat; soil erosion was selected because of its similarity to the idea of disintegration and wearing away. Neither of these comparisons is quite good enough because they lack the idea of transmutation of one substance into an entirely new one. Thus, the transformation of a caterpillar into a butterfly is an analogue for this natural process, while the spewing forth of dandelion seeds resembles U^{235}'s loss of an alpha particle. I haven't found a perfect fit, so teachers can engage in a mixed metaphor or invent a better approximation.

An electric transformer seems a good comparison for leaves in the process of photosynthesis, because both transform energy. An engine that burns fuel oil and converts it into mechanical energy is a bit better because one form of potential energy is transformed into another. However, the solar energy cell more nearly duplicates what occurs in photosynthesis (light energy from the sun striking and being absorbed by tubes in the panel, which circulate water into an underground storage tank where it is later drawn upon for hot water). Here is a closer fit for the model, but not too imaginative because two processes not as disparate, say, as the dandelion is from decomposing uranium, are compared.

These models seem like the most vivid, corresponding processes already existing in nature or created by man. This is what model building is—juxtaposing in our minds different ideas and searching for the hidden likenesses, the creative process Bronowski saw as essential to discovery in science. These likenesses point to the similarities between the movements of an Arctic ice floe and that of the earth's crust beneath; both involve the movement of masses of matter up against each other creating eruptive pressures in the form of hummocks and earthquakes.

Beginning the process of model building might involve working with a vending machine or the SCIS black box. Then teachers can proceed to explore how chemicals bond together or dip into psychology to ask how the conscious and unconscious minds are structured and interact. I vividly recall reading Freud in high school English and toying with various models to explain the structure of the mind. Two developed—the floating iceberg model in which eighty percent of the ice is beneath the surface, is moved by hidden currents, and in a sense controls the size and mobility of that which is visible (or conscious) and the family house model in which the upper floors represented the conscious mind and the basement the subterranean depths of the unconscious, the foundation of all visible structures.

Each of us has undoubtedly participated in similar inventive searches for likenesses.[8] Teachers' searches with students can and should proceed with phenomena for which they have explanations and those for which they do not. Model building is like Shakespeare's attempt to describe the emptiness of life for a man who is about to lose everything—his wife and his newly acquired kingdom—"a tale told by an idiot full of sound and fury signifying nothing."

Kepler searched for such ways to dramatize his perception of planetary motion:

> Kepler felt for his laws by way of metaphors, he searched mystically for likenesses with what he knew in every strange corner of nature. . . .To us, the analogies by which Kepler listened for the movement of the planets in the music of the spheres are farfetched. Yet are they more so than the wild leap by which Rutherford and Bohr in our own century found a model for the atom in, of all places, the planetary system? (Bronowski, 1956, p. 12)

This "wild leap" of the imagination from experience to the planetary model reflects Einstein's process of scientific discovery, his toying with ideas to arrive at the models or axioms from which he drew conclusions. (Holton, 1978, p. 96).

Imaginative powers unite poets, astronomers, physicists, and children at play with their blocks, for each in his or her own way is playing with objects or ideas. All allow themselves flights of fancy at times with the possibility of creating new explanations of their world, inventing and constructing new ideas, or building a sand castle populated by Knights of the Round Table.

COLONIZING SPACE

Imagine you and your students suddenly transported off into space between the earth and moon as pioneers of America's first space colony. Your new home orbits earth at a point known as L5, a point equidistant from the earth and moon. The colony would be constructed from materials brought from earth as well as from the lunar surface. The purposes of such an adventure would be to develop clean solar energy and beam it to the earth in the form of low density microwaves to be converted to electricity.

Solar generating plants could be built from resources located on the moon thereby saving large amounts of money. Launching from the moon to L5 with mineral materials to construct these solar generators could be accomplished at approximately one-twentieth the cost of similar launches from earth. At L5 the pioneers would supplement lunar minerals with resources from earth for construction of the generators.

While in space huge habitats many times larger than the United States' first such station, Sky Lab I, would be constructed. The first one, to be called Island One, could be constructed within a period of six years, would weigh approximately 500,000 tons, and might be spherical or cylindrical in shape. Within this environment and each succeeding one will be man-made ecosystems capable of sustaining life and meeting very specific human needs. The first colony would house approximately 10,000 people; 4,000 would be employed building additional space units, while the remainder would be engaged in producing the solar power stations.

The physicist who dreamed up this highly practical way of providing alternative energy sources, Gerard O'Neill (1976), foresees the interiors of these space habitats in the following terms:

The interior of the colony will be as earthlike as possible—rich in green plants, trees, animals, birds, and the other desirable features of attractive regions on earth. The design would allow a line of sight of at least a half mile, giving the residents a feeling of spaciousness. The landscape would feature plains, valleys, hills, streams, and lakes. The residential areas might consist of small apartment buildings with big rooms and wide terraces overlooking fields and groves. Near the axis of the structure, gravity would be much reduced and, consequently, human powered flight would be easy, sports and ballet could take on a new dimension, and weight would almost disappear. . . .The space colony would have separate residential, agricultural, and industrial areas, each with its optimal gravity, temperature, climate, sunlight, and atmosphere. Intensive agriculture would be possible, since the day-length and seasonal cycle would be controllable independently for each crop, and care would be taken not to introduce into the agricultural areas the insect pests which hamper earth agriculture. . . .Only 111 acres would be needed to feed all 10,000 residents. (p. 28)

To establish all this, asserts O'Neill, would "require nothing new in the way of physical understanding or materials technology."

Naturally, if humans were to establish such colonies, they would be similar to the pioneers of the unsettled, unexplored West. Imagine the problems to be solved by these brigades of explores:

> Design, construction, and operation of solar power plants.
> Transportation of men and materials from earth and moon.
> Design and construction of suitable space habitats to house 10,000 persons.
> Design and construction of a variety of ecological systems within each space habitat to accommodate needs for agriculture, living space, recreational places, and the like.
> Psychological, sociological, economic, and political problems associated with establishing new cities in man-made environments where man has the opportunity to improve upon all that exists on earth, not just environments, but institutions and ways of living as well.

It should be evident that within two decades the possibility exists that man will be conquering the next frontier—outer space—and that in the process problems will have to be solved that involve all areas of human endeavor and inquiry from science to sociology, politics, economics, psychology, communications, arts, and even religion. Remember the work of Metcalf and Hunt in social studies (see chapter II) where "relevant Utopias" were imagined after identifying significantly critical areas of life in need of improvement.

If it is possible to imagine such alternative environments with the real difficulties they present, isn't it possible that most of these problems will be faced and solved by today's adolescents? They are the ones who will be the construction engineers and government leaders in these islands in the sky. Couldn't teachers, then, take flight and fantasize themselves at L5 confronting some of these space age problems, thereby engaging their students and themselves in the scientific processes of observing, identifying variables, developing hypotheses, designing experiments, predicting, and interpreting data? Can teachers create such "an imaginary garden" and study the "real toads" that are bound to emerge? Why not create a pretend outer space world to stimulate students' imaginations and involve them in rational problem solving at the same time?

It seems as if there are innumerable ways of utilizing such an imaginative structure. It might provide problem solving for a single day's activity or an entire unit focusing upon a set of core concepts such as force and motion, radiation, energy, earth and space, astronomy, artificially created ecosystems, the mathematics of geometrical design, the effects upon human and plant life of varying amounts of sunlight, gravitation, or supportive members within the surrounding environment.

Since all problems of science, technology, and human interaction are encountered when pioneers establish colonies of extended duration in space, a logical idea would be to approach them from interrelated points of view, from an interdisciplinary structure. Here are some possibilities:

- Ecological-physical approach in which problems of establishing viable ecosystems within newly constructed habitats are studied. The focus would be upon design and construction of such ecosystems, taking into consideration function and plant and animal requirements for proper balance and support. Concurrently problems of design and construction of the habitat itself or its power plants would be considered, thus focusing upon problems of force, motion, energy conversion and utilization, and problems of mechanical construction.
- Social-ecological approach in which students design the ecosystems in which to live as well as design social patterns of interaction and problem solving, e.g., what rules will be made, how they will be enforced, what institutions would be created to sustain what values and priorities, how people may relate in family structures, marriage, and schools, and similar human problems.

- Physical-mathematical in which students encounter the quantitative solution to problems of motion, force, and energy utilization in the travel and construction associated with establishing the habitats.
- Social-biological-physical-languaging approach in which the social patterns of relating and the biological and physical problems of living in space are utilized to form the stimuli for development of communications skills such as writing, speaking, and listening. Emphasis would be upon improving such skills while thinking creatively about day-to-day life in the habitat, the lives of its pioneers, and the ways in which they deal with their problems.

Creating such integrated structures is very arduous work requiring time for planning and evaluation before, during, and after undertaking such a project with one or more teachers. Additionally, of course, it requires support from school administrators who may have to help create time for such planning and provide assistance in obtaining resources. Without such support, too much of the teachers' efforts will have to be undertaken on their own time.

It is important to note well again, however, that the suggestions offered here are meant as stimuli for thought, and their introduction into the classroom ought to commence on a small scale to determine the extent of student and teacher interest. If sufficient interested is manifested, then, perhaps, larger scale undertakings can be planned with students. Later on I present some different ways in which students can participate in these problem solving activities.

Whether or not teachers undertake to create an interdisciplinary structure and plan only to work with the space habitat notion on a more limited basis, it might be illustrative to present some of the possible problem areas within the grasp of secondary school science students. There has been no attempt to subsume each problem under a specific subject matter category to reflect the relationship of one problem with another:

- Create a livable environment in one L5 colony suitable for animal and plant life. At your disposal are earth soil, lunar soil (containing silicon, aluminum, oxygen, iron, titanium), and any variety of animal found on earth. Decide upon the ecosystem's function, land structure, amounts of water and its configurations, animal and vegetable life, and quantities and support relationships needed. Describe the ecological niche of each animal and plant and how mutualism, competition, support, and balance would be achieved.

- Create a livable environment in another L5 colony, or the same one, suitable for human life. Again, consider functions (residential, industrial, recreational), land topography, soil type, animal-vegetable inhabitants and reasons for your selections, maximum population density supportable, energy resources, utilization of space, heat-light requirements, and amounts and variations in gravitational force, if any.
- After designing one complete ecosystem (or portion thereof) change it significantly for a different colony by altering its significant variables to achieve a different quality of balance within the system or a varied function, e.g., habitation by alternative forms of life, serving divergent purposes. Some of the variables to consider are: water forms and quantities, topography, elements of the biotic-abiotic environment, consumers-producers, atmosphere, gravity, and soil type. This is an excellent opportunity to pose "What if" questions to diagnose and stimulate students' formal thinking capabilities.
- For farm areas determine the most appropriate animals for breeding and human consumption. Within the designed ecosystem what additional plant-animal life is needed to support such breeders? What would be the water requirements? How would this be made available by mechanical means manufacturable in space or transportable from earth? How would disease and pest infection be guarded against?
- Given the chemical composition of lunar soil and earth soil determine the following: requirements for production of water by the colony, processes for creating a stable atmosphere (oxygen or oxygen plus nitrogen), and the composition of the most fertile soil for cultivation.
- Determine how surface water and air at L5 would remain free of chemical impurities. Identify impurities that would cause problems.

- Determine hydrogen and oxygen requirements for creation of sufficient water to sustain 500 workers at L5. Determine sources of elements and chemical processes involved.
- What alternatives to mechanical propulsion by gasoline alone can be invented? Consider all liquid fuels as well as solids and electricity.
- As L5 rotates gravitational forces are induced. How will these forces vary as one moves from outer rim of habitat along a radius to its center?
- Design an engine for surface vehicular travel that would utilize solar energy. What mechanical, electrical, and energy conversion principles need to be considered and how would they be applied?
- In the absence of natural magnetic forces at L5, what forces should be induced for residential-industrial use? Would there be reason to create a North and South magnetic pole? How might this be accomplished?
- Design a satellite solar power station at L5 for converting solar power to microwaves for transmission to earth.
- Determine the solar energy at L5 needed to provide electricity for the entire United States, one state, or a town of 10,000 homes.
- Determine the force necessary to accelerate a weight of ___lbs. from earth into orbit at L5.
- Determine the force necessary to accelerate a weight of ___lbs. while it is in a space habitat of ___ gravitational force (from zero to 100 percent earth gravitational force).

These problems are suggestions to be "rolled around" (Laura's term) in students' and teachers' minds. I have focused upon space travel because it excites me and reminds me of my fascination as a youth with polar exploration. It is proposed as a model for imaginative inquiry and problem solving, not as a completed unit to be transferred into someone's classroom. At best, the questions here might suggest others that teachers and students can play with at the beginning of a unit or a class session.

This brings me to a consideration of how teachers might introduce and sustain a space colony game. Research on teaching has shown that teachers talk more than students, ask more questions, and that most of the talk focuses upon the presentation and recall of factual knowledge.[9]

Yet when teachers ask imaginative questions, more student responses are generated in the form of answers and other questions. If teachers want students to think imaginatively, therefore, they have to ask imaginative questions.

This means that if teachers want to stimulate students' imaginative thinking they must begin with questions that are open ended ("If you lived in a space colony, how would you change schooling, government, or kinds of foods we eat?") and then provide a forum for students to interact with and learn from each other, a process so natural it is hard to understand why we overlook it so often.

Additionally, we must be like the first grade teacher I observed recently who had asked how much two dimes and three nickels and one penny added up to; children gave four or five different answers, and Carolyn Krause calmly and warmly accepted all of them. She *then* proceeded to ask the children how they arrived at their answers, and then, of course, they saw some of their mistakes. "We have two different kinds of thinking here, children," she added as they proceeded to correct their errors. In working with childrens' or adolescents' or adults' imaginative thinking, teachers must be accepting and encouraging of divergence. This is where the science teacher mentioned earlier had some difficulty, but we all do because of our tendency to look for the correct response. What was so fascinating to me about Carolyn was that she was talking with six-year-olds about *thinking;* how many times do high school teachers talk with adolescents in their classrooms about different ways of thinking or how they think about a specific problem?

Teachers need to ask the questions, they must be active listeners and help their students to be the same, and they have to be accepting of some of the wild speculations that will result. This isn't easy, since it requires playing different roles with students—as explorers of the possible—and this takes a lot of time. Once teachers have engaged in such combinatorial play with ideas, as Einstein suggested, then they can begin to think more logically about what is doable, about what the consequences might be.

Here are some different approaches to the space colony game I have found effective in different situations:

- Student task groups for problem solving. Students identify a problem, define its parameters, examine resources, seek alternative solutions, test or simulate testing a solution, and evaluate results. Such small group work is very adaptable to working on a number of different problems by the class as a whole. Problems can be teacher and/or student generated, depending upon student maturity and independence of thought.
- Case study method. Teacher creates a case study that might contain one or several problems to solve. One might concern an environment that failed at L5 with students being asked to seek the causes and recommend improvements. (The breakdown of any system, such as a nuclear power plant or the failure of an innovation in a school, provides similar case study material). Case studies are excellent for small group work and are likely to generate good varieties of alternative solutions; this process encourages peer questioning, suggesting, evaluating, and, above all, listening.
- Independent study and research on a specific problem, e.g., the results of psychological studies of human subjects in isolation such as the Skylab astronauts.
- Small group projects as a culminating activity for a unit or science fair. This might require integration of methods suggested above and require work over a longer period of time. This approach has the obvious advantage of giving students the opportunity to integrate far more information and spend more time in research and problem solving with their peers.

These are viable alternatives to the whole group discussion and to total teacher control of objectives and activities, which is usual in most classrooms. What David and Laura will react to is what a small child enjoys while playing with a good toy—problems or objects characterized by novelty, complexity, ambiguity, and dissonance or incongruity.

What will impede anybody's playing with a toy or a space colony problem is too much control exercised by a parent or teacher. This control is not only exercised over objectives, but can be seen too often in the daily question and answer patterns in classrooms. These patterns usually consist of a teacher asking a question for which there is a one or two word answer; it is the teacher who then reacts to the answer by saying, "Good" or "That's not correct." Too seldom do they turn answers and questions back upon students for their evaluation or for an alternative solution. It's only when teachers do what a seventh-grade science teacher did recently when asked by a young girl, "How *do* you tell the age of a galaxy?" that they encourage productive thinking. He redirected the question back to the students and what ensued was one of the most fascinating examples of students' imaginative thinking and challenging each other about the different ways of thinking about galaxies and their origin. "This could be a meeting of astronomers," Cliff Knapp concluded. And indeed it could have been, because no one really knows the answer to that question. Research indicates[10] that playing the role of an accepting facilitator as Cliff did here can stimulate students' divergent thinking skills.

CONCLUSION

I know how many people are going to respond to what has been suggested—"This all takes so much time and we have to cover too much material. . ." Yes, it does take time—thinking at the higher levels of cognition requires a lot of time. I am certainly not suggesting that any change can be wrought overnight, nor that some of the possibilities presented here ought to be imported *in toto* to classrooms. My objective is to present possibilities and to stimulate the imagination so that teachers begin to see science not as an accumulation of many facts, but as a way of thinking about the world. This demands that we regard ourselves as teachers and our students from a slightly different perspective—not as information dispensers and gatherers but as explorers on the playgrounds of our minds.

Productive thinking, finally, cannot be based upon a restrictive view of the physical world in which efficiency, predictability, and measurability are the supreme values all wrapped up in neat, rational, logical bundles like electrons before Heisenberg developed the Uncertainty Principle. The world isn't like this and neither is the kind of thinking that produced the quark, *Hamlet,* the concept of universal gravity, the Sistine ceiling, the Keplerian laws and *Eroica.*

This kind of thinking is perhaps characterized by a remark David made to me at his Senior Awards Assembly where he received a small scholarship for his musical talents: "I thought at least you would give the Whoopie Award for being at least three standard deviations away from the norm!" Sometimes that's what it takes (together with a little seat power). "This way of thinking," noted Geroch (1976), "implies a greater mental flexibility and a greater tolerance for uncertainty than we tend towards naturally, perhaps."

NOTES

1. See Ley, W. Our earth—by chance. *Science World,* September, 1963, *7,* (1), 4–6.

2. See Johnson, R. (1975). Johnson's survey of research concerned the establishment of meaning as relating a bit of information "to the existing cognitive structures of the learner, i.e., to the residual of his earlier learning. . ." "Meaningfulness" thus becomes the extensiveness of such a "network of referential associations" (p. 427). When the associations or "relational bridge" established is inventive, learning is enhanced (p. 430).

3. See *Omni,* April 1979, *1,* (7), 29.

4. *New York Times,* November 30, 1976. Changes in the earth's angle of rotation are seen as the "fundamental cause of the ice ages."

5. *New York Times,* May 29, 1979, p. C1. Some systems do not degenerate into chaos and disorder but appear to increase in complexity and order.

6. See Herron, J. D. Piaget for chemists. *Journal of Chemical Education,* 1975, *52,* (3), 146–150, for a lucid and extensive comparison of the different tasks performable by concrete and formal thinkers in chemistry.

7. See Taylor, A. M. *Imagination and the growth of science.* New York: Schocken, 1970.

8. See Samples, R. (1976).

9. See Dunkin, B. & Biddle, M. (1974).

10. See Rogers, C. Beyond the watershed, and where now? *Educational Leadership,* May, 1977, *35,* 623–631. Teacher empathy and congruence were reported to improve students' creative thinking performance.

Just as in a game we could by agreement of all players, make different rules under which to play. . .so Euclid could have chosen other axioms.
—Constance Reid (1963)

Programs that provide significant opportunities for exploration, nonverbal expression, laboratory activities and multisensory learning may enable students to reach new levels of mathematics performance.
—Grayson Wheatley (1978)

5

ADVENTURES WITH MATHEMATICIANS

THOSE WHO PLAY any game, be it the numbers, chess, red rover, or uproar, may think it's the only game in town. Soccer was David's favorite game, but he had others, including the one he'd play on his teachers. Sitting in math David sometimes had a newspaper laid out in front of him while the teacher, Mr. Factum, was discussing a formula at the board. The object of the game was to convince Mr. Factum that he wasn't paying any attention to the polygonal perversities to be learned. When so convinced, the dauntless Factum called upon David for an answer expecting a blank stare.

"Oh, let's see," grinned David, "the answer must be, ah. . .a= ½bh." He had won! Factum was chagrinned at having to compliment one of his less enthusiastic mathematicians whose mind works like a tape recorder with two or more tracks. One track is tuned into the sports page and the world of championship soccer;

the other track, with lowered volume, receives Factum's sometimes scrambled signals.

David's mental gamesmanship is similar to the games Laura and others play on teachers: change the subject, change the test date, make the oral reports as long as possible, give me an A even though I haven't done any work, and did the Greeks eat ice cream? David's interest in math is significantly less than Laura's, so he often indulges in note passing with the cheerleader sitting next to him: "Why don't you have a rah-rah tee shirt on like everybody else? Isn't that punishable by death or something?" When the topic of sine and cosine emerges, David jauntily peers out the door looking for the STOP signs advertising the nonlittering campaign for the high school grounds. And when the class is presented with the time and motion problem involving a sailboat leaving Newport at the same time the *Queen Mary* leaves Southampton, he is busily drawing both vessels with imaginary crews darting in and around the scribblings of $D=RT$.

All this tomfoolery may be distracting to Mr. Factum and may keep David from grasping the facts or learning the skills he needs to succeed in math. On the other hand, Grayson Wheatley and his colleagues suggest that David's imaginative playfulness, especially his aesthetic talent, might very well be an entree into the mysteries of mathematics. Indeed, some evidence suggests there are students who will benefit from appeals to their skills in spatial thinking and visualization when logical, sequential thinking does not avail.[1] This research suggests David's interest and performance in math might be positively improved if teachers occasionally appealed to the functions of the brain's right hemisphere instead of continually tapping into those of the left. If they could harness David's considerable imaginative prowess, as well as that of the cheerleader who sits next to him, playing the math game might draw more of his attention than "rah-rah tee shirts"—admittedly, a difficult task!

Laura does not need such alternative strategies, for she is keenly interested in math, and her voice will be heard throughout this chapter. However, for both David and Laura adventuring in their mental playgrounds is bound to enrich and enliven their study of math as well as enhance its meaningfulness. Since the Pythagorean theorem, $a = \frac{1}{2}bh$ and $E = mc^2$, are all products of the imagination, why not avail ourselves of this limitless reservoir of possibilities?

OF MATHEMATICAL MYSTERIES AND PUZZLES

Children playing with a new toy—say a new truck, set of building blocks, or a Jack-in-the-box—are likely to poke, push, and prod it in order to discover what it is. If the toy is sufficiently novel, complex, and different from other toys they have, they'll continue to explore its mysteries and play with it.

Mathematics has long been a field full of such toys, novelties, and puzzles. A story, which may well be apocryphal, is told of Einstein who, as a young lad, cared little for algebra until an uncle showed him how to regard it as a game, "a merry science," in which one played detective in search of an elusive *x*. Much later Einstein was to describe the whole world as a "great eternal riddle" (Clark, 1971, p. 12, 18).

Many lovers of mathematical unknowns have presented us with excellent and fascinating explorations into such mysteries: Martin Gardner's *Mathematical Puzzles and Diversions* (1959); and Kasner and Newman's *Mathematics and the Imagination* (1963). Among the many puzzles mathematicians have created are such intriguing brain twisters as:

A traveler comes to a riverbank with his possessions: a wolf, a goat, and a head of cabbage. The only available boat is very small and can carry no more than the traveler and one of his possessions. Unfortunately, if left together, the goat will eat the cabbage, and the wolf will dine on the goat. How shall the traveler transport his belongings to the other side of the river and keep his vegetables and animals intact? (Kasner and Newman, 1963, p. 159)

An explorer walks one mile due south, turns and walks one mile due east, turns again and walks one mile due north. He finds himself back where he started. He shoots a bear. What color is the bear? (Gardner, 1959, p. 23)

How many colors will be required to color a map, with any number of countries, so that no two countries that adjoin on a frontier will have the same color? (Carroll, 1958, p. 18)

A bag contains two counters, about which nothing is known except that each is either black or white. Ascertain their colors without taking them out of the bag. (Carroll, 1958, p. 18)

Bob wants a piece of land, exectly level, which has four boundary lines. Two boundary lines run exactly north-south, the two others exactly east-west, and each line measures exactly 100 feet. Can Bob buy such a piece of land in the U.S.? (Polya, 1957, p. 234)

Such puzzles and riddles as these may challenge youth and set their minds thinking about the parts of the whole that can be manipulated and the hypothetical solutions to be tested. Sometimes, as in the case of the map problem, computers must assist in the solution, but for others insight and logical thinking abilities are needed.

In my experience as an observer of teachers in various subjects from elementary through high school, I have noticed how the introduction of a puzzle serves as a stimulus for more student involvement and interaction with each other. For example, after reviewing the formulas for obtaining the areas of such shapes as a rhombus, isosceles trapezoid, and triangles, a teacher presented her students with a paper cutting puzzle that confronted them with a basic paradox: the area of the original rectangular shape was 64 square inches, yet when cut into two right triangles and two trapezoids, the combined areas of these four figures totaled 65 square inches.[2]

"Hey! Wait a minute!" exclaimed Laura as she struggled with the seemingly impossible contradiction of the law of conservation of matter. Her classmates, arranged in small groups to figure out this problem, spent a good ten minutes arguing and confronting each other with alternative hypotheses and conclusions. This puzzle stimulated curiosity, just like David's poking into cow barns and kindergartners exploring the ins and outs of a gigantic tirescape in their play yard. And like the social studies teacher's challenge to her students to become church members (chapter II), this puzzle possessed novelty, complexity, and a blatant contradiction to expectations of what should be.

IMAGINATIVE TRANSFORMATIONS

Some of my own initial discomfort with mathematics, especially algebra, may stem from its very imaginary nature. In algebra we create symbols, x and y, to represent unknown quantities and employ imaginary numbers ($i = \sqrt{-1}$) that do not directly correspond to observed experience. I was never able to consider the search for x as a game or even "a merry science" as Einstein did. I wasn't very adept at manipulating symbols that stood for other symbols, and math instruction for me was, consequently, a process of memorizing formulas for different kinds of problems. Geometry was always easier because I could picture the shapes and manipulate them imaginatively.

What might have helped is what Marshall Gordon (1978) calls the "liberating nature of mathematics" contained in its language— "what if" and "suppose." Rephrasing these expressions communicates to students a sense of personal exploration of a problem —"What if *I*" rearrange the givens in this fashion? "What if *I*" toy with them in my mental playground? "It is we who create the world, school, and mathematics," noted Gordon (p. 267), and meaning and power come only when students take control of the elements and reorient them to suit themselves or to find the most useful pathway.

Such personal exploration is exemplified in Max Wertheimer's *Productive Thinking* (1945) in which he describes giving a five-and-a-half-year-old girl a parallelogram after outlining how to obtain the area of a rectangle and asking her if she could find the area of this new figure. This she did by cutting off the left-hand portion—"It's troublesome here"—and placing this triangle on the right-hand portion thus creating a rectangle (see Figure 2).

Figure 2

Another child took a piece of paper cut as a parallelogram, joined the two ends forming a ring and then cut it in the middle. "Then it's all right," she said (p. 49).

What Wertheimer saw as essential elements in these examples of problem solving were "regrouping with regard to the whole. . .reorganization. . . [in which] factors of inner relatedness are discovered. . ." (p. 50).[3] This is not the process of blind recall that Wertheimer would have observed in my learning of algebra. He noted such rigid thinking in another classroom when he presented students with a parallelogram turned on its head; their reaction was, "Teacher, we haven't had that yet," (p. 16) even though they had just learned the formula for the area of this figure.

In the spirit of Wertheimer's gestalt thinking experiments teachers might ask geometry students to consider the following activities for mentally arranging the givens:

- Vary or modify such elements as quantities, relations in space of various geometric shapes, or the shapes of figures themselves, e.g., determine if the area of A is equivalent to that of B (which is obtained by visually rotating one end of A, as in a game of cat's cradle, see Figure 3).

Figure 3

A   *B*

- Following Wertheimer's example, discover the areas of various figures after being given or determining the area of a square, rectangle, parallelogram, triangle, or trapezoid.
- As suggested by Edward de Bono in *Lateral Thinking* (1970), geometric shapes are ideal for playing the game of "What if I. . ." rearrange these parts this way. He starts by asking readers

to generate alternative ways of viewing objects. For instance, an L shape can become a carpenter's angle, a gallows upside down, half a picture frame, or a large rectangle with a smaller one added (p. 70), see Figure 4.

Figure 4

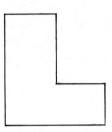

To see all these related objects drawn from previous experience, we must be able to take this L shape and manipulate it visually in our minds. A somewhat more complex exercise is to divide the whole into parts in this manner: divide this square to make an L shape with the same area using only two cuts; see Figure 5.

Figure 5

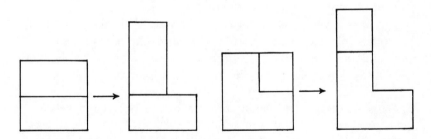

- As a possible introduction to what Kasner terms "rubber sheet geometry" have students cut out a triangle or other shape from a piece of paper and "regroup with regard to the whole" by bending, twisting, and distorting its shape in any desired fashion. What remains constant and what changes? What new shapes are created? What can be determined about the new shapes just created?

Such physical manipulations eventually lead to more difficult mental or visual regroupings. It is in the area of visual thinking that mathematics instruction in schools can draw upon recent research and the ways of thinking of some rather prominent productive thinkers (see footnote 7, chapter 3). It was Einstein who noted the relationship between his scientific thinking and art, "the gift of fantasy has meant more to me than my talent for absorbing positive knowledge" (Clark, p. 87).

EXPERIENCES IN VISUAL THINKING

When we daydream we are thinking visually, and the images we project upon the screens of our minds may be combined in a process of free association—driving home tonight, the car, tennis rackets in the trunk, Saturday's game, last summer's vacation. . . . Or we can focus upon one image and develop its future possibilities —how you will approach a friend to ask for a favor. We know that developing inner resources is important for adolescent emotional strength (Singer, 1976) and that practicing spatial thinking has helped children be more productive in math.[4]

Laura is a very visually oriented person. "I think in pictures," she often told me as she related what a teacher's comment made her think of. The physicist George Gamow also found that imagery was an essential element in his scientific research:

> Gamow possessed this ability to see analogies between models for physical theories to an almost uncanny degree. In our ever-more-complicated and perhaps oversophisticated uses of mathematics, it was wonderful to see how far he could go using intuitive pictures and analogies from historical or even artistic comparisons. . . . His pioneering work in explaining the radioactive decay of atoms was followed by his theory of the explosive beginning of the universe, the "big bang" theory. (Ulam, 1976, p. 183)

Neither David nor Laura is at this moment on the verge of revising either of these theories; however, there seems to be every reason to encourage both of them to more actively use their imagery making capabilities in the following fashions:

> A.M. Turing (1912–54) conceived of developing a machine which could solve a problem of a particular kind, thereby establishing a method for the solution of any such problem. (Reid, 1963, p. 274)

Simple math operations are often approached by using a visual device such as the one in Figure 6. When Laura saw the Turing ma-

Figure 6

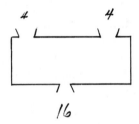

chine, she exclaimed, "This is really excellent. We don't get enough of this." I asked her to apply the principle to any other mathematical situation that came to mind. "Well, O.K., we can make these kinds of machines. . . . (see Figure 7) Can you make

Figure 7

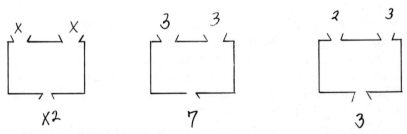

sense of that? First of all, you must see a pattern emerging here. . . . How do we go from the top to the bottom? What you're doing here is trying to figure out what the machine is doing." This is what other mathematicians have termed "rummaging around in your mind to find the important frames" that tell what kind of problem you are confronting.[5]

The Turing machine is like a model of how a particular process works; in this regard it is similar to the SCIS black box (chapter IV) where students figure out how the inner workings of the box operate. A friend of mine, George Magdich, poses this model building problem for his trigonometry students:

> Utilizing any materials you wish, build a model of the wrapping function going from -4π to $+4\pi$.

His students have produced ashtrays, pin cushions, frying pans, and snow tires divided into four quadrants identifying the values of cosine x and sine x for different values of x.

In addition to asking students to create physical models for trigonometric concepts, they can think of pictures and analogies drawn from the world of the visual artist as Gamow did.

- In learning the geometric axioms and theorems, suggest that students seek out visual associations with physical objects, such as bridges, pyramids, space needles, grids, anatomical outlines, spiderwebs, and sea shells of various configurations. For example, the vertical angles found in the game of cat's cradle are a pair of folded arms, interlocking suspension wires on the Brooklyn Bridge, or two dancers bending and touching at the waist.
- "Messing about" with geometric shapes stimulates students to discover required theorems inductively. Suitable and aesthetically pleasing shapes abound in designs found in Persian rugs, the Islamic art of the Alhambra, metallic crystal structures, and the paintings of Escher, Kandinsky, Pollock, Mondrian, Rothko, and Klee. Abstracting shapes from these works of art and twisting them in space as was done with the paper triangle will provide many possibilities for student imaginative thinking.

The human body is a work of art, and teachers can personify mathematical concepts just as they did the egotist and atheist (chapter III). Choreographing a right triangle, obtuse angles, and similar parallelograms with teachers and students enacting Euclid need not require an artist-in-residence to stress the value of personalizing these concepts. What is required is a person like George Magdich who sees value in using what Wheatley calls "multisensory" activities, alternatives to verbal, logical, and sequential learning.

Visual thinking, creating images in our minds and playing with them, can be developed with these kinds of activities:

- Evan Maletsky engages students from junior and senior high schools in an activity called rotating figures in space. Take a square, triangle, or rectangle and rotate it about an axis (through the center or along a diagonal). What figure is created? How many different figures can one create in this fashion? This could be done just by asking students to imagine the rotation, much like the exercises on many aptitude tests where students are required to mentally manipulate a geometric objects.

- Then imagine a more difficult three dimensional object such as a cube and rotate it in your mind, placing the axis in different positions, especially through the center. What figures are created? Given certain dimensions, can you find the volume of the created shapes?

"We don't play such games in order to achieve specific results," Maletsky noted, "but to give students control over the problem."[6] Educators have just begun to acquire some empirical evidence on students' ability to think creatively in mathematics,[7] and one reported aspect is student reaction to being asked to generate as many different solutions as they can. "Is this how we're supposed to do it?" they ask, reminiscent of those younger children who disappointed Wertheimer with the rigidity of their thinking.

I have attempted to arouse the imaginative thinking abilities of students by conducting the following experiment in multisensory visualization:

1. Take any shape currently under study—circle, triangle, rhombus, ellipse, or trapezoid.

2. Picture this shape in your mind—see its outlines in space.
3. Visualize it rotating clockwise/counterclockwise.
4. Make it any color you wish/change the color.
5. Touch it and imagine the texture of its contours.
6. Imagine eating it. What does it taste like?
7. What fragrance does the shape have?
8. See the shape within a three-dimensional space connected to other shapes. Change this shape into any other shape.
9. Change this shape into anything you wish.
10. Imagine what the world would be like without this shape if there were only this shape.
11. Personalize your shape by injecting yourself into the image. What do you see/hear/feel?

In practicing this exercise in ninth and eleventh grade math classes (my friend George's), many interesting responses were heard.

One older girl imagined a triangle: "Light blue and pink. . . .I felt like I was inside one of those spiral swirly things [pin wheel] you hold with a stick and it goes around when you blow it. . . .It tastes like a piece of blueberry pie." What if the world had no triangles? "There would be no bathroom deodorizers that have a triangular shape. . .couldn't make arrows, roofs on houses, dinner bells. . . .We wouldn't have noses."

One younger boy saw a world without triangles as one lacking "pyramids, roof tops, trees, peoples' heads, windows, houses, mountains, and flower beds."

Both students revealed themselves to be quite imaginative judging by the number of answers to the "what if" question. Perceiving the triangularity within the human body was unexpectedly humorous and perhaps is an entrée for using the human body as a geometric laboratory. For a city dweller like myself the emphasis upon roof tops as triangles was a surprise—there are very few dormers visible from where I sit.

When Laura tackled this exercise, she chose a rectangle. She saw it spinning like a pink pinwheel, felt like soft velvet, tasted like ambrosia, and she transformed it into a rectangular solid like the filing cabinet in the office where we were talking. A world without rectangles would give us opportunities to have circular and triangular desks, but rectangles are rather fun to have around in the form of paintings and sheet music and the like. As with all players, Laura sometimes plays the game by her own rules changing them to suit her own perception of the world. "That was fun," she said with her Cheshire grin.

Another unexpected result was interesting. The older students (eleventh graders) generated more answers than the younger ones to the "what if" question. And in the process these older students changed their visual images more often, for example, from imagining a square pizza ("very thick and chewy, you know, Sicilian!") to a square bar of fresh smelling soap. On the other hand, Laura's younger friends generally retained *one* image throughout this experiment. It is fascinating to me to wonder about the developmental changes in imaginative thinking that might be reflected here. The older students seemed able to dream up more possibilities and relate them to more objects from their previous experience, while the younger children appeared to manifest a unidimensional quality of thinking that lacks the abstract thinking ability—developed later in adolescence[8]—to perceive many different aspects or facets of a problem. I would expect the older students who tried this little experiment to be better, for example, at perceiving the complexities of human motivation in discussing a problem in history or literature.

It is also interesting to speculate on the usefulness of such an activity for teachers. How can exercises such as this help in diagnosing students' performance aptitudes and how would repeated visual thinking activities affect the learning of math skills and concepts?[9]

Visual thinking is often fostered by personalizing an object much as a poet does: "O wild West Wind, thou breath of Autumn's being/O thou, who chariotest to their dark wintry bed the winged seeds." To an actor Shelley's treatment of the western wind means entering into the previous life of the character to such a degree that he knows why he is in a scene, what he wants and needs and, hence, all his lines have much meaning. Without such personalization, at least to a moderate degree, the abstract concepts of math may remain for youthful mathematicians parts of formulas to be memorized and recalled rotely and unmeaningfully.

With this thought in mind I asked second graders what their favorite number was? "Seven," replied several children. "Why?" I asked. "Oh, because I'm seven now," they replied with a twinkle in their eyes.

"What would make you angry if you were a seven?"

"Not having any friends. . .Being smaller than an eight."

"What would make you happy if you were a seven?"

"Being added to another seven to make fourteen. . .Being bigger than a six."

Laura latched onto this idea of personalizing math concepts and easily imagined how she would feel.

A tangent of a circle—you never get inside the circle. . .All you could ever do is roll around the outside. . .You're always governed by the circle without being able to get inside. . .always controlled and sometimes frustrated.

If you were x in the equation $x^2 + 5x - 6 = 0$, and there were two values for x—1 and −6—what does that do to you—two different personalities. . .splitting you apart and not setting you equal to zero? What kind of a thing is that to do to an equation, to an unknown?

Laura's voice rose with the feeling of someone who is frustrated with indecision or conflicting pieces of information, each seemingly valid.

I do not possess Laura's talent and interest in math, yet I have occasionally wondered what it would be like to be trapped inside an isosceles triangle. How is life similar to being so walled in by regularity, conformity, and predictability? Probably like learning in a classroom where the teacher makes all the decisions or in a country where individual choice and freedom is severely constrained by a central government. Am I in any way like such a triangle? No, I am more like what happens when one takes an isosceles triangle, transforms it into a towering cumulus cloud, and with a fanfare from a thousand hemispheric trumpets turns the stratospheric winds loose on it for half an hour—the resulting shape is unpredictable and irregular. But the vertices are still there somewhere!

These exercises in spatial thinking, in visualizing and transforming the abstract are meant to enrich the meaningfulness of mathematics, not to arrive at predictable points on a line. They are meant to tap the resevoir of the so-called right hemispheric thinking processes, which are different from the strictly logical, sequential analytic thinking characteristic of the left hemisphere. David is good at visual, spatial thinking, which involves multisensory images, and some practice in this during algebra might have affected his interest (which was not very high) and his performance (which was, at times, much lower than in other subjects).

WHAT IF EUCLID MET A "CHARMED" QUARK?

Ivan Illich (1971) has observed that playing games is a liberating activity because "they heighten awareness of the fact that formal systems are built on changeable axioms and that conceptual operations have a gamelike nature" (p. 81).

There is hardly a more formal system than Euclidian geometry, but suppose some of its most obvious axioms were less than 100 percent true? What if, for example, students were to entertain the idea that two seemingly parallel lines *do* meet somewhere in space. Where would this lead? Would it only serve to confuse them? Or might such a reversal of a common understanding lead David and Laura to consider, however briefly, the characteristics and paradoxes of curved space or non-planar geometry? Might it lead to an awareness that the axiomatic system of deductive logic many of us memorized without question is the product of one brilliant mind and is not, therefore, the only perspective from which to view the world?

Let us imaginatively stand some of these rules on their flat heads, remembering Sutton-Smith's definition of play as a reversal of control from its normal pattern.

The measure of the interior angles of a triangle add up to 180° I asked Laura if she could envision a world in which this was not true, in which the sum of these angles was less than 180°.

"Oh, sure!" she said enthusiastically, her smile broadening with the challenge of doing the things her way. "On a planet where three dimensions are sucked into two dimensions and two dimensional objects become one dimensional. You have two different sets of rules. . . everything three dimensional in our world is flattened out to become two dimensional. . .a triangle is gradually sucked into a point."

Laura's imagination took her off to a fantasy planet much like Abbott's *Flatland* (1929) and similar to the world imagined by the Russian mathematician Lobachevsky (1793–1856). Both Laura's and Lobachevsky's triangle would exist on a "pseudosphere," a shape resembling the bell of a trumpet. Here a small triangle would be nearly flat and contain approximately 180° degrees, but as it increased in size, its interior angles become progressively smaller as does their sum.

"Ever hear of Lobachevsky?" I asked.

"No," she replied with much surprise that someone else had thought of a world different from one constructed of planes as Euclid's is.

In Lobachevsky's geometry other rules prevail:

> Parallel lines never meet but approach each other asymptotically. ("Yeah, like railroad tracks," Laura noted.)
> As a triangle increases in area, the sum of its interior angles decreases.
> For any line L and any point P not on that line, there exists more than one line that contains P and is parallel to L. (Kasner & Newman, 1963, p. 138)

Adventuring from a world where Euclid was turned outside in, we journeyed to another where we turned the former Immutable One inside out.

"Can you picture a world in which there was no straight line containing P and parallel to line L?"

She thought for a while then said, "No, can't see it."

But the German mathematician Riemann (1826–66) could, and he developed an alternative set of geometric game rules that apply on a sphere. For here every "straight" line—the shortest distance between two points—is an area of a great circle that passes through the center of the sphere. Such lines all meet at a north and south pole and cannot, therefore, be parallel to each other. Some interesting and alternative theorems derivable from Riemann's way of looking at the world include:

> The sum of the interior angles of a triangle is greater than 180°.
>
> As a triangle increases in size, its interior angles increase in measure.
>
> From a point *P* not on line *L* any number of perpendiculars can be drawn. (Kasner & Newman, 1963, p. 144)

Thus, people have invented non-Euclidean geometries, those of the pseudosphere and the sphere, and have been able to develop consistent deductive system from them. They succeeded, thereby, in freeing mathematics "from the tyranny of the obvious, the self-evident, and the true." The value of a geometry "is determined within this framework and has nothing to do with 'the truth'" (Reid, 1963, p. 160).

Playing with the rules of a game can produce a different perspective upon the world. By processes of reversal or inversion teachers and students can step beyond the "tyranny of the obvious:"

"If two lines intersect, there is exactly one point at their intersection." What if we say there are an infinite number of points at the intersection? Impossible? Yes, in common sense plane geometry. However, consider the Euclidean definition of a point—something without dimension. Therefore the actual point at which two lines meet can and does cover "an infinite number of mathematical points" (Reid, 1963, p. 130).

To transcend three-dimensional visible space and consider sub-atomic physics for a moment one might say that the space where any two lines meet can be composed variously and unpredictably of nothing or of particles—if a point could be perceived as the equivalent of many such particles in constant motion. Thus, in the Alice–in–Wonderland world of the over 200 known subatomic particles (of which "charmed" and "colored" quarks may be the elementary building blocks) and in accordance with Heisenberg's

Uncertainty Principle, there may or may not be something at the intersection of these two lines in question. The three-dimensional world composed of concrete particles, whose position and velocity are determinable, measurable, and predictable as part of a separate, objective world has long ago given way to one that interacts with the observer, is governed by rules of probability, and is composed of particles that "must not be pictured as static three-dimensional objects, like billiard balls or grains of sand, but rather as four-dimensional entities in space-time." They are dynamic processes, bundles of energy, "continually changing into one another —a continuous dance of energy" (Capra, 1975, p. 203).

Laura felt this inseparability as she pictured the atomic nucleus of hydrogen much in the Bohr planetary model fashion, but she could also imagine herself sitting atop the nucleus peering out upon a whirring electron and feeling anxious and excited as another atom with its energy bundles approached. She imagined herself inhabiting an atomic particle, just as Copernicus imagined himself sitting atop the sun wondering what he would see as he peered out into our solar system. The "objective" world will, therefore, yield to personalization, and this is another dimension beyond that of the fourth dimension of time.

So if plane old Euclid encountered the "charmed" quarks that come in a variety of "colors," we would witness some of those improbabilities and mysteries Einstein thought to be "the fundamental emotion that stands at the cradle of true science. He who knows it not and can no longer wonder, no longer feel amazement, is as good as dead."[10]

CONCLUSION

Mayer (1975) has proposed a three-stage model of the learning process in which there appears to be potential for transferring knowledge to novel situations. The model consists of receiving information, possessing previous related knowledge, and, subsequently and most importantly, searching for related meanings, ideas, and concepts within one's memory. The imaginative activities suggested here and the questions posed to Laura attempt to expand students' thinking beyond the "tyranny of the obvious" and to make more meaningful associations in the process.

If the process of doing math becomes more meaningful and by inference more enjoyable, then perhaps educators have improved math achievement. We need more investigations like those that relate visual thinking to improved learning, especially for students like David and me whose logical thinking skills may be less well developed than our spatial and aesthetic ways of perceiving the world and processing information, especially in mathematics. At times the logic of math is like the flamingo Alice used as a croquet mallet: "Just as she had got its neck nicely straightened out and was going to give the hedgehog a blow with its head, it would twist itself round and look up into her face, with such a puzzled expression that she could not help bursting out laughing. . .a very difficult game indeed" (Carroll, 1960, p. 80).

NOTES

1. Moses, B. *The effects of spatial instruction on mathematical problem-solving performance.* Paper presented at the annual meeting of the American Educational Research Association, San Francisco, April 1979.

2. This example was presented to students of geometry by Frances Palmieri, a teacher intern from Montclair State College.

3. Polya (1957) calls this process one of "decomposing and recombining" significant details or elements of a problem once the problem is understood.

4. Consult Moses, B. (1979).

5. Remarks made by D. B. McLeod concerning *Aptitude-treatment interaction in mathematics instruction using calculators.* Paper presented at the annual meeting of the American Educational Research Association, San Francisco, April 1979.

6. Maletsky, E. Personal communication, April 23, 1979.

7. Brandau, L. & Dossey, J. *Processes involved in mathematical divergent problem solving.* Paper presented at the annual meeting of the American Educational Research Association, San Francisco, April 1979.

8. The growth from concrete to more abstract thought is referred to,

drawing primarily upon Piaget's description. For an example of this transition consult Adelson, J. The political imagination of the young adolescent. In Kagan, J., & Coles, R. *Twelve to sixteen, early adolescence*. New York: W. W. Norton, 1971.

    9. Consult Moses, B. (1979).

    10. "The talk of the town." *The New Yorker,* May 28, 1979.

"Nice? It's the only thing," said the Water Rat solemnly, as he leant forward for his stroke. *"Believe me, my young friend, there is* nothing—absolutely nothing—*half so much worth doing as simply messing about in boats. Simply messing,"* he went on dreamily, *"messing—about—in—boats —messing—"*

—Kenneth Grahame, *The Wind in the Willows* (1940, p. 7)

6

"MESSING ABOUT" WITH TOADS, TAPES, AND BERNINI

DAVID WAS FOND of messing about in just about any kind of boat, canoe, tent, rucksack, or cookware because he was an explorer who had fun being in the outdoors. I once accompanied him on a camping trip to Lake Placid where he tried on a pair of cross country skis for the first time. David was a pretty good track man, but on this occasion he slipped, slid, banged into pine trees along the narrow trails, and fell down on every little slope imaginable. Careening down the bunny slope he invariably ended face down in the snow, feet pointing skyward like two ballistic missiles. He was, indeed, enjoying making a mess of himself and experimenting with the unknown as he often did in school. When confronted with the challenge of doing another report, he wondered what it would be like to teach sixth graders about human and animal adaptation to changing environments, a subject close to the heart of every adventurer. "I did it, I guess, just for the fun of it, for the challenge. . .to do something different."

Messing about with boats, skis, film, or ideas involves momentarily forgetting that there is an objective or destination down river and releasing ourselves to the joy of jumping, sliding, and leaping from one thing to another in an act of exploration and discovery of what may be altogether new destinations on different streams.

David Hawkins has described a way of organizing such a process in "Messing About in Science" (1965), an article depicting fifth graders who were encouraged to play with pendula "exploring differences of length and amplitude, using different sorts of bobs, bobs in clusters and strings, etc." Following the exploratory phase children were guided to prepared instructional materials in areas of their own interest and, subsequently, into large group "colloquia" of children and teachers in which basic questions of theory and abstract thought were consciously raised. Such a curricular framework is similar to one suggested for adolescents by Charity James in *Young Lives at Stake* (1973)—inquiry, making, and dialogue.

The Water Rat's messing, David's slipping and sliding, and Hawkins' experimenting are what scientists and artists do in the initial stages of the creative process, either exploring the unknown to generate a problem or dreaming up solutions. Picasso, for example, delighted in destroying the sketches and paintings created en route to a final product, saving perhaps only the red from one to use in its successor. And Poincare compared his early attempts at solving a math puzzle to rearranging mental atoms (elements of a problem) to find the most elegant and beautiful combination (Ghiselin, 1955, pp. 56, 41). Messing, toying, wandering about are all part of what Laura meant by letting ideas "roll around" in her head.

What I would like is to suggest other areas where students and teachers could profit from having the time, space, and attitudes that would permit sufficient wandering among those things adolescents could enjoyably explore.

VIDEO TAPING

A video tape system seems like a rather intricate mechanism to mess about with. However, one can permit students to create tapes by giving them the opportunity to play with a video camera.

If there is portable video tape equipment available, bring it into the classroom. Place it in the center of the room with chairs in a circle around it if possible. Demonstrate how to start and stop the equipment and how to activate the camera and focus its lens. If you don't know how, invite a media person in to demonstrate or, better yet, pre-select a student to learn how to operate the equipment so she or he can instruct classmates and you as well.

Then ask for volunteers to mess about. You'll need a camera person, someone to watch sound levels (if your equipment is more elaborate than a SONY Portapak, for example), and three or four actors (or players). There are numerous ways to begin and here are some suggestions:

- Narrate a recent humorous incident.
- Complete any values clarification sentence (Were I stranded on a desert island, these are the books, friends, and the like I would want with me. . . .If I had $1 million I'd spend it upon. . . .).
- Imitate various adolescent role types—the jock, the curve raiser, the gear head, the hipster, or preppie.
- Enact a daydream or fantasy (In 20 years this is what I'll be doing.)
- Role play an incident suggested by one of the students.

Once the first group has played out a scenario before the camera, roles can be reversed between actors and technicians or anyone in the class who wishes can volunteer to play out a role or fantasy or express an opinion.

If you are courageous enough, you might leave the room and let students' imaginations take flight. My first experience with leaving students alone to play with media resulted in their imitating before the camera a variety of adults—teachers, "fire and brimstone" preachers, and parents. The tape, which students subsequently shared, revealed students' abilities at imitation as well as their creativity. Their personal identifications were playfully enacted, revealing both their emotional attachments and their facility with abstracting from another person idiosyncratic elements of his or her personality and creatively recombining them according to the imitator's wishes, a process that is often humorous.

In this instance the student acting as a store front preacher decided to concentrate on soliciting money. I never asked why a message about heaven and hell was not included, but I have a hunch that the economic appeal was what left its pinch on everybody's flesh. In the scene the preacher was confronted by a heckler, played by a girl affecting a French West Indian accent. Try as he did there was no convincing this *nouveau arrivee* to contribute her hard earned dollar to his Save the Sanctuary Fund, especially when there was no visible sanctuary. For New York City youngsters this scene was personally most meaningful.

I gave David and his friends in suburbia another Portapak for several weekends because they expressed an interest in dramatizing that state of mind characteristic of the Land of Whoopie. This view of the world of Whoopie revealed itself as a place where schools are at times transformed into animal habitats full of bouncing, screeching animals sneaking up on innocent freshmen who can never determine where the noises come from, where the principal, "Boberoo" Honeysuckle, is concerned with the administration of lockers, where consumers in a department store are as if by wizardry transformed into kangaroos and fourteenth century Gregorian minstrels, and where poets recite works composed with Alice-in-Wonderland logic and are finally stood on their ears by having the camera turned upside down.

In thinking about both these video tapes it occurred to me that it might be significant that inner-city kids chose to satirize a religious aspect of their culture, whereas suburban kids chose the school as the butt of their humor. In both instances, the young people transcended their ordinary roles, restructured situations in accordance with their unique view of the world, and disclosed some of their concerns and identifications.

Messing about with video tape can stimulate an infinite variety of student initiated activities, from creating documentaries of actual conditions in and around schools to serving as the medium for working out personal problems in a manner similar to that created by Winthrop Adkins in his Life Skills Curriculum. One particular problem solving use comes to mind—a colleague and I in an alternative school used video tape to help students think through the need for cooperation and the roles each should play on a forthcoming camping trip. Instant video feedback molded this particular group of campers into a more cohesive entity.

AESTHETICS

Writing in 1917 in *Spontaneous Activity in Education* Maria Montessori revealed her view of the relation between education and spontaneous, idiosyncratic activity.

> Her goal. . .was to educate children and not to let them engage in spontaneous activity. . . . Again like Froebel the materials and techniques of this educational play were fixed and provided little opportunity for spontaneous activity. . .the child appears to have little opportunity for creative activities, nor for peer and social interaction. (Neumann, 1971, p. 21)

What Montessori and Froebel, the founder of the kindergarten in Germany, were more interested in was using such activities as work in clay or drawing to reach adult-generated objectives. For Froebel (1967) "The child's pleasure in drawing develops his desire to shape a whole, to recognize separate parts as constituents of a whole" (p. 116). And for Montessori (1964) work with clay was used as a stepping stone to writing. "Those whose clay work remains unformed and indefinite will probably need the direct revelation of the directress, who will need to call their attention in some material manner to the objects around them" (p. 242). "Messing about" with materials appears not to have been a valued activity *per se*, because of overriding interest in attainment of specific concepts (relation of part to whole, unity in diversity, and so forth) or in the acquisition of specific skills.

Similarly John Dewey could not be perceived as an advocate of messing about, committed as he was to the social usefulness of learning. Dewey's word for messing was "fooling," which he defined as "a series of disconnected temporary overflows of energy dependent upon whim and accident." This was not to be encouraged. "When all reference to outcome is eliminated from the sequence of ideas and acts that make play," he continued in *How We Think* (1933), "each member of the sequence is cut loose from every other and becomes fantastic, arbitrary, aimless; mere fooling follows" (p. 285).

But that's what fooling and messing about *are* all about! And there does appear to be value in just this kind of "fantastic, arbitrary, aimless" fooling in aesthetics. Consider the kindergarten teacher I recently observed who directed (or constrained) the children's imaginative explorations of what a snowflake might look like by shouting, "Snowflakes aren't stars!" There was no potential for the development of children's imaginative powers in that classroom because what mattered was the teacher's intended outcomes —perfect snowflakes for the forthcoming Christmas celebration.

> In or out of 'em, it doesn't matter. Nothing seems really to matter, that's the charm of it. Whether you get away, or whether you don't; whether you arrive at your destination or whether you reach somewhere else, or whether you never get anywhere at all, you're always busy. . . . (Grahame, 1940)

Following Water Rat's advice in matters of aesthetic education there ought to be time just to play with paints, clay, or other media of expression without the ever present press for useable or presentable-to-parents-on-bulletin-boards results. Humanities courses often offered at the secondary school level would appear to be a natural arena in which to engage in aesthetic play. Consider the definition of the humanities offered by Ralph Barton Perry, who stated the humanities embrace:

> whatever influences conduce to freedom. . .any agency or relationship or situation or activity which has a humanizing, that is a liberalizing effect, which broadens learning, stimulates imagination, kindles sympathy, inspires a sense of human dignity, and imprints that bearing and form of intercourse proper to a man.[1]

If there is an activity epitomizing freedom that affects learning and stimulates the imagination, it is play; if there is an activity that embodies the essentials of humanity, it surely is play.

Here are some examples of aesthetic play drawn from two different approaches to the study of humanities—the chronological and the topical.

- In a study of primitive man, play with various natural materials such as fibers, wood, stone, gut, and vegetables as early people might have done in their few idle moments. Potential: how these materials might be combined for self-expressive or utilitarian purposes.
- In a study of the medieval era, play with bits of colored glass. Potential: designs reflecting humankind's expression of the glory of God through light penetration.
- In a unit on scientific discovery, mess about with old clocks and/or watches, exploring their interrelationships and intricacies. Potential: translation to Newton's model of the universe as a gigantic clock set in motion by God and governed by laws of cause and effect.
- During a study of the baroque period, sketch human figures and freely drawn waves, curlicues and circles. Potential: how baroque artists such as Bernini altered the classic Leonardesque human figure.
- Play with complex three-dimensional designs in solid geometry, creating various shapes and combinations of shapes, and examine their beauty and proportion. Potential: imitating some of Leonardo's creative play with such shapes as he was investigating the problems of proportion in mathematics and abstractions in general. These mathematic puzzles intrigued him (as they did Einstein as a youth) and such new interests "always took him back to old familiar ones, enriching his painting and helping him penetrate engineering theory and practice" (Marinoni, 1974, p. 70).[2]
- Mess about with various aesthetic media, materials, and forms, for example, light projected by flashlight, seal beam, or overhead projector through various media such as air, water, prisms, or video camera. Potential: relationships between medium, func-

tion, and form in studies of aesthetics, the artist in society, or
varieties of aesthetic expressions.

- In examining the world's religions, play with various symbols,
  rituals, and meanings in an attempt to understand human kind's
  confrontations with the unknown and the varieties of solutions
  represented in different religions.

- In studying man and society, play with social organizations and
  institutions and establish new forms with different purposes and
  constituencies. Such play could be in the form of pre-packaged
  board games such as Life Career and Diplomacy[3] or it might
  take the form of teacher-prepared simulations in which students
  are confronted with new environments (such as the space colony
  in chapter VI) and are asked to create organizations to meet
  specific needs. Another method would be to follow the Metcalf-
  Hunt relevant utopias paradigm.[4] Potential: we realize the truth
  of Harvey Cox's observations that, "In play we see the boundaries set by the political structure as something human beings
  create in their attempts to cope with reality. When I play I know
  I am more real than the rules. . . .Even if I'm prevented from
  doing so, I know it *could* be done, that the game is not eternal or
  immutable" (1973, p. 185).

- In investigating man and nature, fool with certain natural laws
  by posing this question: "What if we were able to override, overcome, supercede, or otherwise negate this particular law? How
  might it be done and what might be the consequences?" Playing
  with seemingly immutable laws in this fashion potentially leads
  to an understanding of the way certain scientists have imaginatively confronted nature and generated useful and novel approaches. For example, James Clerk Maxwell conceived of a way
  of overcoming the second law of thermodynamics by inventing a
  magical demon that would prevent a system from attaining a
  state of maximum entropy without doing work. Such questions
  can, of course, also be asked about our understanding of natural
  phenomena: "What if the sun doesn't revolve about the earth?
  What if. . . ?" Potential: engaging in "combinatory play" with
  ideas that have led to so many fruitful reinterpretations of the
  structure of our universe.

In his letters on aesthetic education the German poet Friedrich Schiller, reacting against Kant's subjection of aesthetics to "judgment," felt that man achieved his quintessential humanity in the free interplay of his two main drives—that of the senses and that of rationality. "In the act of escaping from the serious pull of thought and feeling to a mental state which satisfies both without succumbing completely to either, he finds an analogy to the act of playing," wrote Calvin Thomas in 1901. For Schiller only man knows how to play and "only in playing is man completely man" (p. 281). Playing embodies man's essential freedom, freedom which in 1795 Schiller felt was being imperilled. Thomas Mann (1959) once observed that Schiller displayed an "eternal boyishness" and "delight in an exalted game of cowboys and Indians" (p. 11).

The humanities in secondary school (or elementary, for that fact) offer excellent opportunities to exemplify Schiller's famous observation, to give students the experience of engaging in the essential characteristic of humanity—"combinatory play" with objects, ideas, functions, and meanings, free from constraint and the need to produce useable results. All the ideas, concepts, skills, or solutions to problems people investigate playfully are creations and inventions of the human mind. This is as true in poetry as it is in science, as true for social organizations such as marriage, schools, and representative government as it is for models of DNA and an expanding universe.

The humanities offer the unique experience of spanning many traditionally isolated and separate domains of inquiry in an attempt to discover man's essential humanity, those human actions that exemplify freedom and liberation from social, emotional, physical, or spiritual constraints, burdens, or illusions. If people are free and completely human in their play, it may be because in play they are in total control, deciding what is meaningful, and behaving like persons who make things happen in their lives.

NOTES

1. Quoted in *The humanities, a planning guide for teachers* prepared by

The University of the State of New York, The State Education Department, Bureau of Secondary Curriculum Development. Albany, New York: 1966, p. x. See also Dudley, L. and Faricy, A. *The Humanities*. New York: McGraw-Hill, 1960.

2. See Gardner, M. (1959).

3. See Boocock, S. & Coleman, J. (1970).

4. See chapter II.

7

PLAY AND THE
PROBLEM OF CHANGE

YES, PLAY REQUIRES time, free time to explore and invent; it also requires toys to play with, space, and supportive adults or playmates. And time currently is at a very high premium in schools when one considers the demands of parents for concentration upon essential skills and improvement of test scores, of administrators for attending to the needs of students with special needs (the handicapped and the gifted and talented), of board of education reductions in services, which often increase teacher-pupil ratios and eliminate valuable programs, such as some of those in the arts. These are some of the grim realities in an era where economic pressures to conserve are constraining budgets and expectations. Concurrently there are political pressures to produce and to prove to the public that teachers are being effective, efficient, and professional.

With all these pressures and constraints where is there time to play? Time is a dimension, a human construct, and what is important is not that it keeps passing but how it is used. There are three major reasons why I think it is important for teachers to find the

151

time for imaginative thinking in classrooms.

First, if we look at students in classes we find that in addition to paying attention to the teacher's objectives, they find time for many other activities—daydreaming, cleaning out notebooks, chatting with their friends and telling stories, inventing excuses for leaving class, scribbling notes to each other, and playing the game of "let's get the teacher off the subject so we can do what we want." In other words, no economic, political, or social pressure exists that can prevent students from using their imaginations for *their own* purposes. Why not channel some of this energy and inventiveness into helping teachers achieve some of their objectives? When students become disinterested, they play—this means they face a problem of occupying their time, and their solutions are very often novel, e.g., communicating daily with fellow students who occupy the same room at different times by writing messages on the desks, messages that very often reflect their passionate attachment to one kind of music or another such as "Zappa lives forever" or "Disco is Dynamite." They communicate in pictures and symbols of their culture as well; a red tongue found on many desks throughout David's and Laura's school represented The Rolling Stones.

The point is students use time in class as they choose—to pay attention to subject matter presented by the teacher or the subject matter they bring with them in their dreams, their yearnings to communicate and establish connections with friends, and their searching for and experimenting with different roles to play.

Secondly, teachers cannot afford to overlook students' imaginativeness because what stimulates much of their doodling, daydreaming, and dialogue is boredom. Boredom reflects an attitude, and educators know that how students feel about a subject, a teacher, and the school significantly affects their learning. They also know that students who are involved in learning will achieve significantly better results after instruction (Bloom, 1976). It makes sense, therefore, to tap students' imaginative thinking if only to involve them and to affect the way they feel about a subject. Without such opportunities for inventiveness, Davids and Lauras will turn to their own concerns, and teachers will have failed to marshall all the resources available.

And, finally, teachers must find the time because they cannot afford to be totally reactive to pressures beyond the school walls. They are ultimately responsible to parents, but this does not mean that they abdicate their responsibility to provide a meaningful education. This entails transcending the achievement of high test scores to include the development of those human capacities and talents that differentiate people most from animals. Acquiring specific skills and knowledge is important, but so is fostering tasks requiring imagination. Teachers can and must begin to perceive education as a process that focuses upon both and schools as one of the environments in which to do both.

There is evidence accumulating that indicates that a high grade point average is no guarantee of ability to cope with the realities of adulthood. Achievement of good grades in schools does not necessarily lead to the ability to establish intimate relations with people, to cope with change, or to earn a high salary.[1] We need more studies like that of Vaillant (1977), which have identified what he terms mature defense mechanisms that help people adapt to life, e.g., altruism, humor, suppression, anticipation, and sublimation (p. 386). I think imagination is definitely fundamental to almost every one of these mature ways of adapting to life.

In the end, then, teachers *can* take the time to play in classes because students do it all the time, because teachers can foster their own objectives through imaginative activities, and because schools can actively develop the skills and talents that constitute what Lewis Mumford called "a fully dimensioned" human being.

BASIC PRINCIPLES OF CHANGE IN SCHOOLS

"Everytime we play a little game in class or do something that's really fun, I feel a little guilty," Laura said one day as we were discussing the contents of this book. "It's the old Puritan ethic— work versus play." She is well aware that her teachers have to cover material and will be defensive when the principal enters the room with a quizzical look on his face. How can it be educational if it's fun?

These old conflicts between work and play—the resistance of

teachers and supervisors and the apprehension about the unknown —can be confronted if educators attend to specific principles of successful diffusion of change in schools that have been established through empirical research:[2]

1. Identify a real need for change.
2. Involve the participants in shared decision making during the planning, implementation, and evaluation phases of the change.
3. Identify sources of support among people with similar values.
4. Plan how to deal with resistance.
5. Start small; start cautiously.
6. Clarify and make known intentions and intended outcomes and how they will affect life in the classroom.
7. Realize that meaningful change often demands a reorientation of the roles to be played by teachers and students.
8. Evaluate in terms of intended and unintended outcomes and establish feedback mechanisms to alter and adapt the change to meet the evolving needs of students.

These stimuli, processes, and products of change are initial points for further consideration. Each has significance for inducing Davids and Lauras to explore their imaginative potential.

Identifying a Need

Too often educators, including myself, have seized upon an innovation because it was sweeping the country. Attempting to be in the vanguard of educational change, I have, in the past, latched onto a solution for which I never identified a real problem—introducing modular scheduling within an alternative school was an example.

The need for imaginative activities stems not only from a desire to avoid boredom but from teachers' real concerns about how to establish a meaningful connection between their subject matter and the lives of students—students who can't imagine the life of a young Richard Wright, students who are concrete thinkers and can't visualize density or a "charmed quark," students for whom FDR represents only a list of legislative actions taken during the first 100 days, and students (like me) who have great difficulty conceptualizing time and motion problems and adapting one solution strategy to a slightly different problem. Such immediate instructional needs can and should be addressed through some of the kinds of activities suggested in the previous chapters.

Richard Carlson's (1965) diffusion strategy includes as its priority that participants must perceive the "relative advantage" of using an innovation compared with previous practice. How is it better? It's better to have students who are active, inventive, and in control of their thinking processes. It's better when students are relating the important experiences in their lives to the content under discussion. It's better when they perceive teachers as people with imaginations who can do more than solicit facts and their reproduction on examinations.

Finally, the real need and advantage stems from people's desire to control their immediate environment and at times to transcend its limitations or to restructure it in accordance with their own needs. Human beings, whether students or teachers, feel this need daily and act upon it through graffiti on desks, conversations with friends, stories told and invented, roles played out, decisions contemplated and made, and dreams enacted or deferred. The need, therefore, is instructional, curricular, and intensely human.

Shared Decision Making

There is enough research on change in schools to be able to state the obvious—people with a voice in decisions that will directly affect them will be far more interested in working toward meaningful outcomes than those for whom decisions are made by others and passed, usually down, to them.[3] At times we all must surely resent the control exercised over us by others as well as by events. This was the initial and immediate attraction to the playful process for me—*I* am in control.

The implications for play in classrooms require students exercising greater control over the ways they act upon content, which for Piaget is how learning occurs. Recalling information is important, yet acting imaginatively upon it not only aids recall, but may increase the transferability of knowledge and skills to new situations.[4] Shared control of decision making in schools means identifying problems and alternative solutions with peers, a task that requires much patience and listening to each other. When engaged in "what if" imagining, role playing, model developing, or language creation, teachers and students must listen to the other players. Through active listening they can produce more ideas and more associations than if they rely solely upon their own experiences.

Shared control means, finally, that we, the teachers, relinquish and provide more time and space for students' exercise of imaginative power. David's and Laura's musings over "Suppose all the ice in Antarctica melted" required time, and few people could respond, "Venice would no longer be unique" without time to think. It has recently been suggested by Gage (1978) that this is why teachers see so little evidence of the effect of "higher order" questioning on student achievement—it takes time to imagine possibilities.

Be that as it may, relinquishing control, even partially, will always be an emotionally threatening action for teachers, because so much of the process of schooling supports their playing the role of absolute monarch or captain of the ship. For this reason change must proceed slowly, and it proceeds more successfully if the participants are mutually supportive of each other.

Time and Support

Too many educational innovations are attempted on a grand scale, involving everybody without a prerequisite pilot testing on a small group and then gradually extended to more and more participants over a long period of time. The approach to play must be similarly cautious; start slowly and in small portions like feeding a child his or her first bites of asparagus. Children are more flexible than many adults—or so it seems. However, because other Davids and Lauras have never been challenged to role play in English or history during high school, their first attempts with friends will need much support from you. Students love to imitate and clown around at times, but doing it at a teacher's request in front of peers will require the emotional reinforcement a mother gives her 12-month-old son when he goes off to explore new toys in a strange playroom.

Davids and Lauras need emotional encouragement and so do teachers. One of Kurt Lewin's major premises about how people willingly undertake to change their behavior was that it would occur successfully within a mutually supportive group possessing common goals and values (Benne, 1976). Therefore, teachers who attempt the novel require friends of similar persuasion who can empathize and help them over the rough spots. Finding a core support group of people of similar values and perspectives who have successfully experimented with change is very important. No one enjoys being out on a limb alone, especially when the economic and political winds are gusting as they are today. "Being playful," David noted, "can be rather lonely."

Resistance

But what if the child does not like the asparagus? What if your students try a role playing session once, fool around, and from all appearances seem to have felt it was a waste of time? "Is this going to be on the test?" they may ask in derision. Should or do you mark it off as a failure never to be tried again? That's one unfortunate response of some teachers. Another approach, however, is to sit back and analyze the situation to discover why you observed the results you did. Remembering that anything as strange as role playing in a science class among adolescents is bound to raise several eyebrows, teachers ought to examine the failure from several perspectives, e.g., students' familiarity with such activity, their ability to experiment with the unknown, and the preparation and communication of the intent or potential value of the experiment. Too often teachers fail to reflect upon what they have done in the classroom to determine why an activity succeeded or did not. Self-reflection upon what actually occurred within a class is one of the keys to professional growth, for without it we muddle along without acquiring understanding about why events occur as they do. Only through difficult introspection with ourselves and our students can we grow and be liberated from the routines and roles we play daily.

Since so many of these imaginative activities are really liberating in the sense that they transcend the "givens" in a situation, teachers will have to lead the way by shedding some of their emperor's garments and be the first one to play a different role or think aloud about what would happen if three numbers could be added simultaneously rather than just two. Only when students know that their teachers are not demi-gods imposing inevitable rules upon them, will they be able to reflect upon Euclid, Einstein, or a Warriner grammar book as open to change. Playing with Euclid's theorems and postulates gives the idea that his is not the only math in town, that there are options and the possibility of looking at the world through a different set of glasses.

So begin to allow a few minutes at the beginning of a tenth-grade science course for students to look at, touch, and "mess about" with a set of balances or pendula or a model of the atom. Then as Laura feared, the supervisor or the principal walks in, and the teacher becomes apprehensive about what's going on. "The teacher would probably immediately send everybody back to their seats and go onto something else," she added, reflecting how much she has learned over the years about the potential value conflicts existing between her teachers and their supervisors. I shouldn't have been amazed to hear her say this, but I was. Thinking that such conflicts were revealed only in conferences between adults, I neglected to consider the messages adults convey daily and the lessons students learn as they watch adults interact in schools. Laura's perception was one of the unanticipated outcomes and, therefore, part of the "hidden curriculum" of our schools.

But what do teachers say to a supervisor who is genuinely surprised that they are experimenting or are not at the prescribed point in the textbook? Here are some suggestions I have found practical:

- Be as certain as you can of the significance of the activity—its potential for student growth and development of attitudes, skills, or concepts as well as its research outcomes, if available.
- Be able to integrate an experiment or novelty within your own curriculum—know its relation to your goals and objectives. For

example, I use role playing in graduate courses because it helps me dramatize and vivify critical concepts and attitudes and it may reveal to students some of their real concerns.

- Be willing to stand back and observe the results of your experiment and share them with others. Too often we participate in what Matthew Miles (1969) called "role performance invisibility" and "lack of interdependence" among faculty members. Share the success and or failure with the supervisor for purposes of improvement.
- Know how the approach or activity can contribute to the improvement of student participation and how this relates to improved student achievement (Bloom, 1976).
- Be familiar with others' perspectives and criteria and adopt their point of view. "Imagine the real" situation of the supervisor; slip into the garments that reflect his values. Such imagining is good in conflict resolution situations. The point is to examine what you do from the standpoint of a potential critic and find some common ground. The strict disciplinarian can only be impressed if students are *more* orderly while sitting in small groups working diligently.
- Be open to constructive evaluation—there is seldom only one way to solve a problem.

Resistance to change is always present for a wide variety of reasons. Forging ahead without considering who among students, faculty, and administration might raise what kinds of problems is proceeding with blinders on and ignores much of what is already known about the successful planning and implementation of change in schools.

Outcomes

Oftentimes educators undertake an innovation such as contract learning or team teaching without a clear idea of exactly what the intended outcomes are. How will life in classrooms be different? How will students and teachers relate to each other after the change? (Sarason, 1971).

The problem with play, of course, is that it will be very difficult to judge its effectiveness by the usual kinds of paper and pencil tests. How, for example, does one know the significance or effectiveness of a person's daydreaming or role playing? Or how does one measure ability to play with ideas and judge the outcomes of such mental gymnastics? Play is a process that potentially produces new ideas or solutions; it may have few immediately discernible results.

Educators will have to look at such possible meaningful areas as how much time students spend on word play, their changing attitudes toward the subject and the teacher, the kinds of risk they are more willing to undertake, and the quality and variety of ideas and questions they generate.

Play potentially generates new personal meanings for all players, and ultimately we have to ask them how it has been important. I asked David this question after observing his playful behavior for eight months, and he said my attention had made him much more aware of the significance of his creative talents—"It was O.K. to be a little weird. . . ." He was far more accepting of his own artistic and verbal abilities and felt less uncomfortable with his lack of a gift for math and science. Somehow schooling had given him the feeling of not measuring up to his friends who were more talented in these subjects. He now had a more balanced self-perception.

Perhaps asking students to visualize models and fictional characters and to daydream will result in their perceiving playful behavior as important and as part of their personal repertoire of skills that will make their lives much more worth living.

CONCLUSION

As Laura so perceptively noted, it will be very difficult to convince her teachers that there is value in daydreaming and in experimenting with rules and roles in play situations. This is especially true during times when social and political forces press educators toward accountability in the rather narrowly constrained curricular areas of composition, computing, and comprehension.

However, their posture should not be one of passive acceptance; on the contrary, David's and Laura's imaginative behavior is a treasure to be discovered, cherished, and nurtured for its positive

benefits during their growth and development as thinking and feeling people. "All this is so important," noted Laura. "It really has
to start in the kindergarten." Only when educators begin to support children's playfulness from kindergarten through high school
will the adult years of the Davids and Lauras of this world be characterized by a maximum heightened ability to act with vision and
adaptive flexibility to physical, social, and intellectual challenges.
The problem of play is not with David or Laura, but with the adults
who supervise and guide their education. The adults who choose to
see classrooms as primarily environments for the transmission of
accepted knowledge without opportunities for fantasy and experimentation will always constrain students' natural talents and,
thereby, their growth.

With such a narrow perspective David will continue to observe as
he did to me one day that "It's a shame school has to interrupt my
education." Whether or not he had read George Bernard Shaw is
not as relevant as the incisiveness of his perception of his daily encounters in classrooms.

NOTES

1. Fiske, Edward B. High marks seen as no guarantee of later success. *New York Times,* June 5, 1977. Fiske cites research by Douglas H.
Heath: "Maturity and competence in later life seem to be positively cor-
related with 'nonacademic' factors such as character development, moral
values, and 'the empathic skills necessary for understanding and relating
to others.' "

2. Refer to Sarason, S.B. (1971) and Carlson, R. (1965).

3. Refer to Berman, Paul et al. *Federal programs supporting educational
change* (Vol. 7) *Factors affecting implementation and continuation* (R-1589/7-
HEW). Santa Monica: Rand Corporation, 1977. See also *Teachers College
Record,* 1978, *80,* 1, 69–94.

4. Refer to Mayer, R. (1975).

8

PLAY AND CURRICULUM

WHAT DOES LAURA'S admonition suggest for the curriculum of her school and for the school she entered as a very young child? Does a concern for play mean that educators are using it as a means to an end, however valid, real, and necessary these ends or goals may be? I think not.

Play discloses certain processes, themes, and values that are too often overlooked and denigrated by schools and I would like to focus upon several of these and to suggest specific curricular alternatives.

EXPLORING THE UNKNOWN

Play is often an exploratory activity in which children examine Jack-in-the-Box toys, and if they are complex and intriguing, the children will investigate them for a while and find pleasure in playing with them. David exemplified this exploratory zeal, this desire to find new and different ways to solve problems in and out of school. He typifies Erikson's role experimentation in seeking out new experiences—hitchhiking through unknown territory, jumping freight cars en route to Chicago, and making films in history class "for the fun and challenge of it."

162

Upon his return from his first semester in college, I asked him what went through his mind when he confronted a task, particularly in school:

Well, first of all you have a goal, perhaps to get an A. But you have to add onto that other goals. . .like making it fun, making it a real challenge to do. Then you might want to try out a different medium like TV or film, something you haven't done before. . . . What's important to me is expressing myself and to do this you have to let your imagination go. . .take what you perceive and do something wild with it.

Doing something "wild" is David's way of restructuring the elements of a task to suit his need for personal expressiveness, and this is how he makes so many of his personal and academic tasks into real adventures involving risk and confrontation with the unknown. Because he used his imagination when thinking about how to travel through New England and how to do his history assignment, David experimented and played many different roles.

Several weeks after speaking with David, I ventured down to Virginia with Laura. We went there to explore a Walden Two community with a group of her friends who had read Skinner's book and were curious about how the idea had been translated into reality. While there the thought occurred to me that her school might sponsor her attempting a similar experiment, say for one or two months, just as it sponsors AFS and the Experiment in International Living. The challenge would be trying a radically different new life style, one of sharing work, play, possessions, and decision making with about 80 people, in a community where waste, wealth, and poverty are eliminated by cooperative planning that increases "the feeling of freedom" (Skinner, 1948, p. 219).

Why can't schools, as part of their optional curricular programs, offer students the possibilities of investigating alternative living patterns, alternative learning environments where, through short-term internships, they play different roles for the fun and challenge of confronting the unknown? The risk, of course, is that they might discover more meaningful roles than the ones their schools and suburban communities have introduced them to, but that's what happens when fledglings leave the nest. I am suggesting that schools foster living and learning in different nests.

Walden Two communities, IBM, off-off Broadway theater, veterinary medicine, investigative journalism, canoeing down white water rapids, and teaching in elementary schools are all possible alternative environments that might be sponsored by a "walkabout" kind of experience. The "walkabout" is the Australian aborigine's transition-to-adulthood trial in the outback, and Maurice Gibbons (1974) has described a way of thinking about the possibilities of such an experience for secondary schools. Others[1] have made similar suggestions that focus upon the school as only *one* of a wider diversity of settings in which youth become familiar with adult living patterns and career choices.

I think David's and Laura's experiences in extra school settings suggest the real possibility of providing their friends with the challenge and novelty of discovering alternative living and learning patterns that *may* alter the way they think about themselves, their future careers, and education in general.

"LETTING YOUR IMAGINATION GO"

Recently I helped a kindergarten teacher in David's and Laura's district rearrange her classroom physically.

> Now here is where I'd like the math corner. . .over there the reading circle. . .and let's see, perhaps the gross motor skills next to that wall, and the fine motor skills over here. . . .

"Where's the play corner?" I asked after a short while. "Oh," she paused for a second, "over there by the window where the little stove is." She hadn't forgotten it, but clearly what came first in her mind were the subject areas the children required to succeed in first grade. And on up the educational ladder it goes, right up through graduate school and the Ph.D.

Educators only think of play and imagination after all the critical subject areas have been attended to, after the so-called "basics." Even in kindergarten the play corner is losing out to preparing children for first grade academically. One of the consequences of what Dewey (1963) called the fallacy of perceiving education primarily as a preparation for the future is that educators lose sight of developing children's abilities to enjoy the present, in this case through their imaginative play.

Where in our kindergarten through twelfth grade curriculum do educators consciously foster what goes on in the play corner—the pretending, the visual thinking and fantasizing, the metaphor and model building, the generation of possibilities, creating and responding to implausible and hypothetical questions, the going "wild" David mentioned? These are developable skills inherent in problem posing and solving, not only for scientists and artists, but for people in any human endeavor.

If schools are at all interested in the human development of their students, I think they must attend to the activity of play and to the playful approach to life exemplified by David and Laura. If they are interested in students' becoming more than outstanding performers on achievement tests, then they must attend to the play corner, with all its mystery and magic. If educators are interested in their students' becoming people who have an ability to react with unique responses to ever changing situations and becoming more adaptive, then there must be a play corner and a play time in every classroom and in every school.

WHOOPIE AND THE GOD OF THE FIVE PARAGRAPH ESSAY

As David explained in his earlier comments on how he makes a challenge out of routine assignments, everybody has imagination and this, to him, means that everyone perceives the world differently. What's fun and risky is to "take what you perceive and do something wild." And in wildness we find what is so important to David —finding a way to express himself. This personal expressiveness is the essence of Whoopie's differences with the God of the Five Paragraph Essay. In the latter students express their opinions about what somebody else—Hemingway, Shakespeare, or Roosevelt— has said or done. In the Land of Whoopie there are opportunities to express uniqueness through a variety of media—writing, film, cartoons, drama—and in so doing establishing one's own creative voice and, as David suggested, acting upon one's idiosyncratic ways of perceiving the world.

If educators are interested in such personal expressiveness, I suggest that schools prepare composition guides not only for expository writing but for the more personally expressive kind of writing often called creative writing—the *Five Paragraph Expository Essay Guide* and the *Whoopie Guide to Going Wild*. For every expository essay there ought to be an opportunity to play imaginatively with facts and ideas. "Once you've proven you can do it the conventional way," David noted, "you ought to have the opportunity to explore the alternatives by using your imagination."

TICKLING THE TIGER

After returning from our visit to the Walden Two community, I asked Laura what she had learned. Her first answer dealt with the way people lived and the kinds of differences she noted between her life and theirs.

"What was the next most important thing you learned?" I asked.

"That Mr. Barnett was ticklish," she added without hesitation. Her recalling the ride in the back of the station wagon brought forth the smiles and laughter she so often manifested in and out of class. She had attacked Mr. Barnett's ribs with parries and thrusts, much as David did with his friend on crutches. Her tickling proceeded to such an extent that when the car stopped for a late dinner and most of the students had moved toward the restaurant, there was Laura sprawled over the back seat with Mr. Barnett lying on the ground next to the door rolling in laughter. Laura was playing a very nontraditional role for a student—controlling a teacher by incapacitating him with laughter.

What this has to do with curriculum is not that teachers and students should spend time tickling each other's fancy but rather it concerns role reversal, an essential process in play. When children play, they take control of a make-believe world in a way they cannot in the real world. This is exactly what people do when they daydream.

Because schools are so dominated by adults in terms of curriculum, instruction, administration, and management and because adolescence is a period when young people are experimenting with different roles and establishing their independence from adults in their families, where do students find opportunities to practice taking control? Where do educators encourage the kind of role reversal evident in play situations? Alternative schools are appropriate settings for experimenting with student control of objectives, activities, evaluation, administration, and decision making, but this kind of experimentation can be attempted in traditional classrooms as well.

I once asked a group of students in another school about the games they played, leading them to consider what games are composed of, e.g., rules, roles, resources, pay-offs, and rituals. Then I asked them how they thought the game of "teachers and students" ought to be played. Their replies focused upon ideal role models for each to play, and they expressed a rather strong feeling for sharing some control with teachers. In addition to asking that they be perceived as individuals (and not as "so-and-sos sister!") they were, in effect, asking for teachers who could "imagine the real" world they lived in. They talked about altering, if only slightly, an imbalance in the control patterns most often found in schools—teachers speak and students are spoken to.

Teachers often hear it said that students don't have any idea of what is important to study. There is much truth here, but they ought not to hide behind such declarations for they prevent them from listening to students' voices at other times. Sarason (1971) makes a very interesting point in his discussion of the "constitutional issues" in the classroom when he notes teachers' reluctance to share even a modicum of control because of a feeling that students aren't interested or cannot act responsibly. On both counts my experience suggests the contrary.

David and Laura have on numerous occasions related to me their very strong convictions that teaching is a "give and take" situation with teachers and students listening and learning from each other.

Their highest regard is for adults who can imagine the other side, as Buber (1965) suggested was the essence of dialogue.

Sharing control does not mean handing over a class to the students. It does mean, however, that teachers look for opportunities to encourage those students who are able to experiment in safe, secure settings with taking some control of objectives, activities, and evaluative procedures. Government and management can also be included as areas in which students are encouraged to play different roles in schools.

Watching David and Laura challenge accepted rules and roles, crack jokes, imitate dancers and karate experts, daydream, and restructure the conventional to suit their imaginative needs means to me that they derive great joy out of being in control and transcending the limits of a situation. Knowing what frustration results on those occasions when I, as an adult, feel out of control makes me all the more concerned with nurturing within David and Laura and their friends the confidence that results from experimenting with taking control of one's life in different situations, in and out of school.

CURRICULUM AND THE SISTINE CEILING

I often conceive of the curriculum as a series of engagements with stuff, or content, characterized at one end by very tightly controlled structure and at the other end by openness and informal structure. The teaching and learning of introductory skills such as comprehension, computing, and composition are done well with a high degree of teacher control and structure, whereas fostering independent learning through internships, independent study, and individual contracts requires more student control of objectives and activities.

D. E. Hunt's studies (1975) have demonstrated that some students require more adult control and structure than others; this he has determined through an assessment of their levels of conceptual thinking. The objective in education ought to be to help students achieve ever greater degrees of independent thought and action as they progress through the grades. Presently David and Laura are capable of exercising a rather high degree of independence in their learning situations.

In thinking about structure I often consider educational environments as children's toys full of novelty, complexity, incongruity, or dissonance, all of which generate exploration and questioning.[2] A good toy also is characterized by openness; like a block it can be transformed into anything a child wishes. Teachers foster such openness in the curriculum when they encourage students to act independently, to take control, and to use their imaginations. I believe all students can act upon content in this way at appropriate times. Emotional maturity level, interest in subject matter, and developmental level or stage of thinking are important variables to take into consideration for each student.

But for Davids and Lauras, once the concept of the atom has been introduced and mastered, let them create their own models of this invisible phenomena in ways that are meaningful to them, just as they do with poetry, painting, cartooning, pretending to be FDR in the 21st century, or Holden Caulfield in a space colony.

Another way of visualizing the curriculum is to study Michelangelo's Sistine ceiling and to notice his artistic growth from the *Drunkenness of Noah,* the first panel, to the *Separation of Light from Darkness,* the last. Michelangelo commenced this work during the High Renaissance, and by the time he had finished, he had explored a new expressive style to be known as Mannerism. The scene depicting Noah is rendered with clearly delineated lines leaving little to the viewer's imagination regarding the nature of the characters and the action i.e., a very tightly controlled structure. In approaching the separation scene, on the other hand, the artist loosened the structure by leaving to viewers' imaginations exactly how to interpret the scene i.e., lines are blurred, and it looks almost like a picture of God creating Himself. Viewers must use their own experiences, values, and unique ways of perceiving the world.

Curriculum, then, can be viewed as engagements with reality along a continuum from very tight teacher control with little student input to a looser structure with much more student-and-teacher-negotiated input. Once certain skills have been mastered, once the ideas and concepts have been introduced and have become familiar, then teachers can do what Thomas Green (1968) has suggested—invite students to play upon the jungle gyms within their minds.

The question teachers have to ask themselves is whether or not there exists an appropriate balance in our curriculum between *Noah* and the *Separation,* between the precision and predictability of spelling bees and times tables and the more imaginative and idiosyncratic toying with objects and ideas in the playgrounds of our minds.

NOTES

1. See Coleman, J. *Youth, transition to adulthood: Report of the Panel on Youth of President's Science Advisory Committee.* Chicago: University of Chicago Press, 1974. See also *The education of adolescents: The final report and recommendations of the National Panel on High School and Adolescent Education* (HEW Publication No. 76-00004). Washington, D.C.: Department of Health, Education, and Welfare, 1976.

2. See Ellis, M.J. *Why people play.* Englewood Cliffs, N.J.: Prentice-Hall, 1973.

To play is to participate in an event that takes place by chance, entails risk,
and is of remarkable import; it is to have an adventure.
—Robert Neale (1969, p. 43)

9

PLAY AS ADVENTURE

FROM THE DATTNER playground to the executive suite
or the captain's stateroom we embark upon many journeys leaving
one known port and setting a course upon uncharted oceans for a
hoped for destination. Like Columbus and the Apollo astronauts,
we have some idea of what we might encounter along the way, but
inevitably there are surprises, dangers, and serendipitous rewards.

And upon arrival we may discover that the anticipated terrain is
somewhat different from our expectations; it may be a serene haven
in which we luxuriate and sport about with ease and confidence, or
it may be a far rockier coastline requiring that we seek alternative
landing sites and establish our base camp in an unanticipated fashion.

Each journey is an adventure, born of chance or determined
planning, yet born in our imagination from innumerable possibilities involving choices for roles we wish to play during transit and
upon arrival at the final port of call—an occupation, a change of
habit, a new theory, friend, or lover, or just a friendly chat over
coffee with a unicorn. Some journeys are more exciting than others
because there is more challenge—the peaks we are scaling are entirely unknown and far steeper than any we have encountered pre-

171

viously. And each journey shapes our lives a little differently, and here is the value of play and playfulness—within our imaginations we create the form and substance of our lives.

A journey of a foot or one thousand miles begins the same way Christopher Robin set out upon so many of his—with a game he called chairs. There are four chairs in Christopher's nursery, and the game is to decide which to sit in. If he occupies the first, he is an adventurer exploring the Amazon River; if the second, he becomes a sea captain sailing upon the world's oceans; and if the third, he would become a roaring lion in a cage.

> Shall I go off to South America?
> Shall I put out in my ship to sea?
> Or get in my cage and be lions and tigers?
> Or—shall I only be Me? (Milne, 1924, p. 20)

His problem is what he wants to be for the duration of the game. It is the same problem confronted by Holden Caulfield as he explored the seemingly labyrinthian maze of adolescence attempting to find his niche, his identity, the role he will play in the game of life:

> I got bored sitting on that washbowl after a while, so I backed up a few feet and started doing this tap dance, just for the hell of it. I was just amusing myself. . . .I started imitating one of those guys in the movies. In one of those *musicals*. I hate the movies like poison, but I get a bang imitating them. (Salinger, 1951, p. 29)

Both Christopher and Holden were playing a game. Adults tend to be amused by Christopher's game because he is a young child and to be tolerant of Holden's perhaps because they know such imitations and playfulness are temporary and soon they will find themselves and lead productive, working lives.

But the essence of the games they play is engaging what is meaningful in their lives and in a pretend context controlling their interactions with others and with new and exciting roles, rules, and outcomes. Christopher may never become a great sea captain or an explorer of South America, but that is not the point. He is being himself and shaping himself for the future. In his playing with the dangers of the Amazon or with the thrill of command, he is toying with associations and identifications that are potent for him now. So is Holden playfully amusing himself to the delight of his friend, Stradlater, but he too is toying with attractions and significant occurrences in his life. He says he hates the movies, but his fondness for imitating them and playfully embellishing his remembrances with idiosyncratic gestures, words, and actions reveal just how meaningful they, as well as the heroes portrayed therein, are to him.

Christopher and Holden and David and Laura are engaged in the adventure of life, setting forth as did Stephen Dedalus who broke away from his Irish background, his family, the church, and his parochial schooling to live the life of the artist and "to recreate life out of life" (Joyce, 1956, p. 172). This is the potential of play—"to recreate life out of life" and in the imaginative encounters with the toads or meanings within that life to fashion for ourselves a new being. Life is a process, a process of change, not a static entity. As such play is, as Schiller has noted, that quintessential human activity where through internal command *we* create and recreate the being of ourselves. In play we transcend the real world, the immediate world of concerns and constraints. In freedom and in total control of our imaginative explorations and meanderings we learn that we can take charge of our destinies, we can be that ship captain, the movie idol, or the artist who, in the smithy of his soul, creates the uncreated conscience of his race. In such transcendence is the adventure, challenge, and risk of play.

AFTERWORD

LEARNING IS an amazing process, for the ways in which we learn are as varied as the subjects of our attention. However, there is a certain uniformity of teaching technique used by most instructors which restricts the myriad ways in which we *could* learn. This drastically reduces the inherent excitement of learning new things. Education should be an adventure, not a chore.

When we are in the classroom, as instructor or as student, the opportunity to learn is there. Whether or not we grasp this opportunity and make use of it depends on our state of mind. Are we stimulated, our curiosity aroused? Or are we being doled out information by someone who is as bored as we are? As an instructor, have we left open the channel for two-way communication, or have we fallen prey to the frequent notion that those we teach are there to accept, not share in information?

Humor and playfulness are effective means for obtaining knowledge. They can make learning painless by involving minds and spirits in a sense of adventure. Imagination is necessary for creating engaging learning opportunities and such imaginativeness, when used properly, can foster trust and respect between teacher and student.

DAVID

BIBLIOGRAPHY

Abbott, E. *Flatland, a romance of many dimensions*. Boston: Little, Brown, 1929.

Abt, C. *Serious games*. New York: Viking Press, 1970.

Algeo, J. Portmanteaus, telescopes, jumbles. *Verbatim*, 1975, *2*, 1–2.

Arendt, H. Thinking—II. *The New Yorker*, November 28, 1977, 114–163.

Asimov, I. *Fact and fancy*. New York: Avon Books, 1972.

Barbour, I. G. *Myths, models and paradigms*. New York: Harper & Row, 1974.

Benne, K. The processes of re-education: an assessment of Kurt Lewin's views. In W. Bennis & K. Benne & R. Chin & K. Corey (Eds.). *The planning of change* (3rd ed.). New York: Holt, Rinehart & Winston, 1976.

Bloom, B. *Human characteristics and school learning*. New York: McGraw Hill, 1976.

Bloom, B. *Taxonomy of educational objectives*. New York: McKay, 1956.

Boocock, S., & Coleman, J. Games with simulated environments in learning. In M. Miles and W.W. Charters, Jr. (Eds.), *Learning in social settings*. Boston: Allyn & Bacon, 1970.

Bronowski, J. *Science and human values*. New York: Perennial Library, 1956.

Bronowski, J. *The identity of man*. New York: Natural History Press, 1971.

Brozan, N. A lift for underprivileged girls: Fantasies of bright futures. *New York Times*, March 26, 1977, p. 9.

Buber, M. *The knowledge of man*. New York: Harper & Row, 1965.

Capra, F. *The tao of physics*. Berkeley, CA: Shambhala, 1975.

Carlson, R. *Adoption of educational innovations*. Eugene, OR: Center for the Advanced Study of Educational Administration, 1965.

Carroll, L. *Pillow problems and a tangled tale*. New York: Dover, 1958.

Carroll, L. *Alice's adventures in Wonderland and through the looking glass*. New York: New American Library, 1960.

Center for Unified Science Education. The dimensions of scientific literacy. *Prism II,* spring 1974. Box 3138, University Station, Columbus, Ohio, 43210.

Clark, R. *Einstein: the life and times*. New York: World Publishing Co., 1971.

Coleman, J. *Equality of educational opportunity*. Washington, D.C.: Office of Education, U.S. Department of Health, Education, and Welfare, 1966.

Cooper, H.S.F., Jr. A resonance with something alive—II. *The New Yorker.* June 28, 1976, 30–61.

Cox, H. *The seduction of the spirit*. New York: Simon & Schuster, 1973.

de Bono, E. *Lateral thinking: Creativity step by step*. New York: Harper & Row, 1970.

de Mille, R. *Put your mother on the ceiling*. New York: Viking Press, 1973.

Dewey, J. *How we think*. Boston: D. C. Heath, 1933.

Dewey, J. *Education and experience*. New York: Collier Books, 1963.

Drew, R. F. The truth of your art is in your imagination. *New York Times,* August 15, 1976, p. 5.

Duberman, M. *The uncompleted past*. New York: Random House, 1964.

Dunkin, B., & Biddle, M. *The study of teaching*. New York: Holt, Rinehart & Winston, 1974.

Einstein, A. Letter to Jacques Hadamard. In B. Ghiselin (Ed.), *The creative process*. New York: New American Library, 1955.

Elkind, D. *Children and adolescents*. New York: Oxford University Press, 1974.

Erikson, E. Identification and identity. In P. Svajian & Z. Cantwell (Eds.), *Adolescence: studies in development*. Itasca, IL.: F. E. Peacock Pub., 1974.

Espy, W. *An almanac of words at play*. New York: Clarkson N. Potter, 1976.

Farb, P. *Word play*. New York: Bantam Books, 1974.

Fergusson, F. (Gen. Ed.). Preface in *Twelfth Night* (The Laurel Shakespeare). New York: Dell, 1959.

Friedman, M.S. *Martin Buber: The life of dialogue.* New York: Harper & Row, 1960.

Friedman, N. *e.e. cummings—the art of his poetry.* Baltimore: Johns Hopkins University Press, 1960.

Froebel, F. *Friedrich Froebel: A selection from his writings* (I. M. Lilley, Ed.). Cambridge: Cambridge University Press, 1967.

Gage, N. L. *The scientific basis of the art of teaching.* New York: Teachers College Press, 1978.

Gardner, M. *Mathematical puzzles and diversions.* New York: Simon & Schuster, 1959.

Geroch, R. What physicists do: Neaten up the cosmos. *New York Times.* June 12, 1976, p. 23.

Ghiselin, B. *The creative process.* New York: New American Library, 1955.

Gibbons, M. Walk about. *Phi Delta Kappan.* May, 1974, pp. 597–602.

Gordon, M. Conflict and liberation: Personal aspects of the mathematics experience. *Curriculum Inquiry,* 1978, *8,* 251–271.

Gordon, W. J. J. *Synectics.* New York: Collier Books, 1961.

Grahame, K. *The wind in the willows.* New York: Heritage Press. 1940.

Green, T. *Work, leisure, and the American schools.* New York: Random House, 1968.

Hawkins, D. Messing about in science. *Science and Children,* 1965, *5,* 5–9.

Haynes, N. L. (Ed.). *Biological science: An ecological approach* (Biological Sciences Curriculum Study). New York: Rand McNally, 1973.

Heidegger, M. *What is called thinking?* (J. Glenn Gray, trans.). New York: Harper Torchbooks, 1972.

Heisenberg, W. *Physics and beyond.* New York: Harper & Row, 1971.

Holton, G. *The scientific imagination.* Cambridge: Cambridge University Press, 1978.

Hubley, J. (Producer). *Everybody rides the carrousel.* Santa Monica, CA: Pyramid Films, 1976. (Film)

Hughes, H. S. *History as art and as science.* New York: Harper & Row, 1964.

Huizinga, J. *Homo ludens: A story of the play element in culture.* Boston: Beacon Press, 1950.

Hunt, D. E. Person-environment interaction: A challenge found wanting before it was tried. *Review of Educational Research,* 1975, *45,* 209–231.

Hunter, M. *Encounter in the classroom.* New York: Holt, Rinehart, & Winston. 1972.

Illich, I. *Deschooling society.* New York: Harper & Row, 1971.

Inhelder, B., & Piaget, J. *The growth of logical thinking from childhood to adolescence.* New York: Basic Books, 1958.

James, C. *Young lives at stake.* New York: Schocken Books, 1973.

Johnson, R. Meaning in complex learning. *Review of Educational Research,* 1975, *45,* 425–460.

Joyce, J. *Portrait of the artist as a young man.* New York: Viking Press, 1956.

Kasner, E., & Newman, J. *Mathematics and the imagination.* New York: Simon & Schuster, 1963.

Koestler, A. *The act of creation.* New York: Dell, 1964.

Levinson, D. *The seasons of a man's life.* New York: Alfred A. Knopf, 1978.

Lewis, N. *Word power made easy.* New York: Doubleday, 1949.

Lieberman, N. *Playfulness: Its relationship to imagination and creativity.* New York: Academic Press, 1977.

Mann, T. *Last essays.* New York: Alfred A. Knopf, 1959.

Marinoni, A. The writer—Leonardo's literary legacy. In L. Reti (Ed.), *The unknown Leonardo.* New York: McGraw-Hill, 1974.

Mayer, R. Information processing variables in learning to solve problems. *Review of Educational Research,* 1975, *45,* 525–542.

McKim, R. *Experiences in visual thinking.* Monterey, CA: Brooks Cole Publishing, 1972.

Mee, C.L. Jr. The last European war. *Horizon,* 1976, *18,* 104–105.

Merleau-Ponty, M. *The primacy of perception.* J. M. Edie (Ed.). Evanston, IL: Northwestern University Press, 1975.

Metcalf, L., & Hunt, M. Relevance and the curriculum. In E. Eisner and E. Vallance (Eds.), *Conflicting conceptions of curriculum.* Berkeley, CA: McCutchan, 1974.

Miles, M. *Learning to work in groups.* New York: Teachers College Press, 1959.

Miles, M. Planned change and organizational health. In F. Carver & T. Sergiovanni (Eds.), *Organizations and human behavior: Focus on schools.* New York: McGraw-Hill, 1969.

Milne, A. A. *When we were very young.* New York: E.P. Dutton, 1924.

Montessori, M. *The Montessori method.* New York: Schocken Books, 1964.

Morison, S. E. *The Oxford history of the American people.* New York: Oxford University Press, 1965.

Mosher, R. L. (Ed.). *Adolescents' development and education—a Janus knot.* Berkeley, CA: McCutchan, 1979.

Neale, R. *In praise of play.* New York: Harper & Row, 1969.

Neumann, E. *The elements of play.* Unpublished doctoral dissertation, University of Illinois, 1971.

Novak, M. *Ascent of the mountain, flight of the dove.* New York: Harper & Row, 1971.

O'Neill, G. Space colonies: The high frontier. *Futurist,* 1976, *10,* 25–34.

Piaget, J. *Genetic epistemology.* New York: W. W. Norton, 1971.

Polya, G. *How to solve it.* New York: Doubleday Anchor, 1957.

Raab, S. Roots of teenage violence. *New York Times,* August 2, 1976.

Random House dictionary of the English language. J. Stein (Ed.). New York: Random House, 1967.

Reid, C. *A long way from Euclid.* New York: Thomas Y. Crowell, 1963.

Ritter, R. *The mystical volcano of Heineken.* Unpublished paper, 1978.

Sagan, C. *The cosmic connection.* New York: Dell, 1973.

Salinger, J. D. *Catcher in the rye.* New York: Bantam Books, 1951.

Samples, R. *The metaphoric mind.* Reading, MA, Addison-Wesley, 1976.

Sarason, S. B. *The culture of the school and the problem of change.* Boston: Allyn & Bacon, 1971.

Schiller, F. *On the aesthetic education of man.* Ed. and Tr. by Elizabeth Wilkinson. Oxford: Clarendon Press, 1967.

Shakespeare, W. *A Midsummer Night's Dream.* New York: Dell, 1959.

Shenker, I. Historians still debate the meaning of the American Revolution—if it was a revolution. *New York Times,* July 6, 1976, p. 13.

Singer, J. *The Inner World of Daydreaming.* New York: Harper & Row, 1975.

Singer, J. Fantasy: The foundation of serenity. *Psychology Today,* July 1976, pp. 32–37.

Skinner, B. F. *Walden two.* New York: Macmillan, 1948.

Smilansky, S. *The effects of sociodramatic play on disadvantaged pre-school children.* New York: John Wiley, 1968.

Sutton-Smith, B. The useless made useful: Play as variability training. *School Review*, 1975, *83*, 197–215.

Thomas, C. *The life works of Friedrich Schiller*. New York: Henry Holt & Co., 1901.

Torrance, E. P. *Thinking creatively with words*. Lexington, MA: Personnel Press, 1966.

Ulam, S. *Adventures of a Mathematician*. New York: Scribner's, 1976.

Vaillant, G. *Adaptation to life*. Boston: Little, Brown, 1977.

Vygotsky, L. S. Play and its role in the mental development of the child. *Soviet Psychology*, 1967, *5*, 6–17.

Wertheimer, M. *Productive thinking*. New York: Harper & Brothers, 1945.

Wheatley, G., Mitchell, R., Frankland, R., & Kraft, R. Hemispheric specialization and cognitive development: Implications for mathematics education. *Journal for Research in Mathematics Education*. 1978, *9*, 20–29.

Whitrow, G.J. (Ed.). *Einstein—the man and his achievement*. New York: Dover Publications, 1967.

Winne, P.H. Experiments relating teachers' use of higher cognitive questions to student achievement. *Review of Educational Research*, 1979, *49*, 13–50.

INDEX